Source Code Seeking on the Web:
A Survey of Empirical Studies and Tools

Rosalva E. Gallardo-Valencia and Susan Elliott Sim

Many Roads Studios

Toronto

Canada

M4N 2S2

http://www.manyroadsstudios.com

ISBN 978-1-304-69545-1

TABLE OF CONTENTS

Chapter 1: Introduction

"I do believe, however, that information technologies (computers and communication networks) are bringing about qualitative changes in how we learn and work. In particular, our abilities and capabilities to seek and use information are strongly influenced by these environments." Marchionini, 1997.

The Web and its associated technological resources are changing the ways people gather and access information. The Web is impacting our everyday life activities ranging from finding driving directions to finding specialized medical information. This impact also includes the ways professionals perform their work. The main reason for this impact is the huge amount and diversity of information that the Web makes accessible.

The Web facilitated the fast pace growth of the open source, which is the practice of distributing source code along with the executables of a computer program. The Web and open source together make available a huge amount of source code that could be reused as is or integrated to create new software. Open source has had a great impact in the development of modern software. Gartner estimated that by 2012, 80% of all commercial software will include elements of open source technology [18]. Not only is the availability of open source code increasing, but also its quality. Recent reports on open source have shown that the overall integrity, quality, and security of open source software is improving [11]. In addition to the open source movement, the appearance of Web 2.0 has increased the amount of source code that is shared on the Web among developers such as tutorials, source code snippets, bug fixes, among others.

Having all this source code available on the Web can make us see the Web as a huge source code repository [27], which developers include in their daily work activities as an important source of information to learn new concepts just in time, clarify current knowledge, or to remember details such as code syntax [4]. Developers are looking for source code on the Web as a technique to write source code. We will call this phenomenon "source code seeking on the Web." We do not use the term search because we want to also include the stages where developers identify the need for source code and use the information found on the Web. It is important to understand how developers look for source code on the Web so that tools and approaches can be suggested to better support developers' needs.

Different models of information seeking have been proposed for different professionals [15, 56, 63], including developers [5, 42], and professionals using electronic environments as an information source [39]. However, there is no model to describe the source code seeking behavior of developers on the Web. We propose such a model to describe the activities involved in source code seeking from the point of view of the developer. This model has five stages. In the first stage, developers identify a source code need that motivates them to seek source code. In the second stage, developers choose a web resource to start the search. Then, developers translate their need to a form that the web resource can process and execute the search. The fourth stage includes evaluating the results given by the web resource to determine which results are relevant and suitable for the task at hand. Finally, in the fifth stage developers use the suitable result to integrate it to their own source code or to get an idea from it.

We use this model to review the empirical studies done to developers, and for the tools that support developers looking for source code. We apply our model to answer the following questions:

- What are the source code needs that make developers look for source code on the Web? How well do the tools help developers identify their source code needs?

- Which Web resources software developers use to start looking for source code on the Web? How well do the tools help developers select a Web resource to start looking for source code on the Web?

- How do developers translate their source code needs to Web resources? How well do the tools help developers translate their source code needs?

- How do developers evaluate the source code candidates to determine which is the most relevant and suitable for their source code needs? How well do the tools support developers in evaluating and selecting the most relevant and suitable result for their source code needs?

- How do developers use source code found on the Web? How well do the tools support developers to use source code found on the Web?

Applying our model to empirical studies of developers and tools that help developers seek source code makes it evident that there is a lack of empirical studies that help us understand all five stages of the source code seeking process. In particular, more studies are needed to understand how developers evaluate candidates and how they use the source code from the Web. Our analysis also shows that there is a lack of tool support to help developers identify a source code need, evaluate results, and use source code found on the Web.

The rest of the book is organized as follows. Chapter 2 presents a definition of source code seeking on the Web and an overview of the proposed model for analyzing this phenomenon. Each stage of the model will be covered from Chapter 3 to Chapter 7. Thus, Chapter 3 will describe the empirical studies and tools that support the stage of identifying of source code need. Similarly, Chapter 4, 5, 6, and 7 will discuss the stages in which developers select a Web resource, translate and form need to a Web resource, evaluate results, and use suitable results correspondently. Chapter 8 includes a discussion of the results after applying our model to empirical studies and tools. This chapter also sketches our future work. Finally, Chapter 9 concludes our book.

Chapter 2: Source Code Seeking on the Web

2.1   Definition

Source code seeking on the Web involves the search, evaluation, and retrieval of source code from the Web, as well as, the application of the retrieved source code to solve a software development problem.

Developers rarely create software systems from scratch. They rely on existing libraries, APIs, or snippets of source code. These existing pieces of software can be found in local repositories and also on the Web. The increased availability of open source projects on the Web and the willingness of developers to share snippets of source code have made the Web the largest repository of source code. Developers frequently use the Web to look for source code that helps them solve a software development problem such as finding the right API to use or finding the implementation of a search algorithm. Source code seeking goes beyond just searching for source code on the Web and includes the evaluation of the source code in the search results, the retrieval of relevant source code, and also the application or integration of the found source code to the developer's task at hand.

Information seeking of developers has been studied before [42] to better understand the process that developers follow to look for information while doing a maintenance task. In contrast to our approach, they did not study the Web as a source of information and they did not focus solely on source code search.

2.2   A Model for Source Code Seeking on the Web

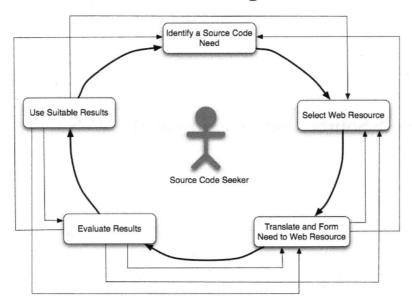

Figure 1. Model of Source Code Seeking on the Web

A model may be described as a framework for thinking about a problem [64]. The model presented in Figure 1 provides a framework for source code seeking on the Web. This model emphasizes the important role of the person seeking source code, the searcher or seeker, whose decisions are influenced by many factors along the process. Other models have also showed the seeking process from the user's perspective [33]. Our proposed model has five stages. The process generally starts when the seeker identifies a source code need such as looking for the implementation of an algorithm or trying to remember the syntax of a programming language statement. The seeker decides that using the Web can satisfy the need for source code. Depending on the selected Web resource, the seeker translates the need to a web resource in the form of a query or browsing a web resource. The web resource returns the results and the seeker will evaluate the results to determine if any of the them is relevant and suitable for the source code need. Finally, the seeker will retrieve and use the suitable results to solve the software development problem that brought about the source code need.

Seeking source code on the Web is not a linear process. Results from any of the stages can cause the seeker to return to any previous stage. In Figure 1, the solid arrows represent the common sequence of stages followed by the source code seeker and the light lines represent the feedback loops that could make the seeker return to a previous stage. In some cases, some stages can be skipped, for instance, when developers use recommendation systems to find related source code on the Web. Depending on the features offered by the recommendation system one or more of the following stages could be omitted: identify a source code need, select Web resource, and translate and form need to Web resource.

The emphasis of the model is on the seeker and not on the system. For that reason, the system or system's actions such as executing query or showing search results are not shown. Similarly, the model emphasizes the Web as the information source used to find source code. However, other information sources such as local source code repositories, documentation, and colleagues can also be used during the process and can influence the code seeking process on the Web.

The model assumes that the seeker is the person who needs to look for source code and is not an intermediary. The model also assumes that Web resources can have different ways to interact with the user in addition to query formulation. For that reason the stage is called Translate and Form Need to Web Resource and not formulate query.

Several concepts and models in different areas of research have influenced the proposed model. A summary of the models is given in Table 1. These areas include Information Behavior, Information Seeking Behavior, Information Searching Behavior, Information Retrieval, Consumer Behavior, Human-Computer Interaction, and Software Engineering. The relationships between most of these areas are shown in Figure 2.

Information Seeking Behavior is concerned with the variety of methods people employ to discover and gain access to information resources [64]. Humans purposely engage in information seeking to change their state of knowledge [39]. Information Behavior includes information seeking, as well as, unintentional or passive behaviors to acquire information such as glimpsing or encountering information, and purposive behaviors that do not involve seeking such as avoiding information [6]. Information Behavior is a subset of Human Communication Behavior, which has a strong focus on the communicator and the channels of communication. In contrast, Information Behavior puts more emphasis on the communication recipient. Consumer Behavior is one area of research in human communication behavior relevant for our investigation [53].

Information Search is a subset of Information Seeking and it is concerned with the interactions between information users and computer-based information systems [64]. Information Retrieval systems are an instance of these computer-based information systems. These systems support the process of searching, exploring, and discovering information from organized data repositories to satisfy users' information needs [68]. Many of these information retrieval systems are also available on the Web.

Human-Computer Interaction (HCI) is the study of people, computer technology, and the ways these influence each other [13]. The goal of HCI researchers is to determine how they can make computer technology more usable by people. Due to the fact that all the areas mentioned before can use computer systems to support their processes and usability is an important concern for all these systems, we draw HCI cross cutting all the previous research areas. However, HCI is not limited to only computer-based systems used for human communication.

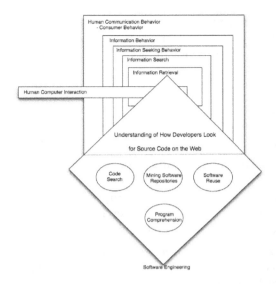

Figure 2. Areas of Research that Influenced the Model of Source Code Seeking on the Web

Software Engineering is the application of a systematic, disciplined, quantifiable approach to the development, operation, and maintenance of software; that is the application of engineering to software [61]. Software engineering is used to create the computer-based systems to support the area of human communication and sub-areas. For that reason, Software Engineering has been draw as a slice of the previous areas, including HCI. It has an overlap with HCI because HCI researchers also investigate the usability of software used by software engineers. The sub-areas of software engineering that have influenced our model include: information retrieval, software reuse, code search, program comprehension, and mining software repositories. Software reuse is the process of finding and using existing components or libraries in the creation of new software [32]. Empirical studies [59] have shown that software reuse is one of the motivations that developers have to seek source code on the Web. The sub-area of code search tries to understand the activities and motivations developers have to look for source code. Code search typically occurs within an Integrated Development Environment while working on the source code for a single project. This activity is often done during the development and maintenance of software, and involves searching for specific program elements in a software project. Developers have mainly four motivations to search for pieces of software: defect repair, code reuse, program understanding, and impact analysis [50]. The sub-area of program comprehension focuses on the cognitive theories that help us understand how programmers comprehend software in a single body of source code and on the tools that aid users in their comprehension tasks [54]. During source code seeking on the Web, developers need to understand the code retrieved in the result set to decide if a match is relevant and suitable for the task at hand. The sub-area of mining software repositories studies the ways in which the mining of software repositories such as source control systems and bug tracking tools, can support the maintenance of software systems, improve of software design and reuse, and support developers and manager's decisions [20]. For source code seeking on the Web, the Web is seen as a software repository that we mine to find the appropriate piece of source code.

All the previous areas contribute to different aspects of our understanding of how developers look for source code on the Web. The area of Information Seeking helps us understand the ways in which developers can purposely look for source code using different communication channels. Human Information could also cover the cases in which developers find information without looking for it, for example when developers use recommendation systems. The area of Consumer Behavior provides clues about how developers decide between different search results and also about the different factors that affect their decisions.

The area of Information Search, specifically Online Information Search, provides empirical data about user's information needs; the process users follow while searching for information, and information use. The area of Software Engineering provides instances of situations in which developers have source code needs and what should be the intended use of the source code. HCI contributes with usability requirements for the systems that support developers while seeking source code on the Web.

Next, we describe each of the stages of our Model of Source Code Seeking on the Web as well as the factors that influence the seeker's decisions and activities during the search process.

Table 1. Summary of Models that Influenced the Model of Source Code Seeking on the Web

Model	Author	Area	Phases	Main Concepts / Phases	Informed by
Berrypicking Model	Bates, 1989 [2]	Online Search	No	- Evolving search - Search process follows a berrypicking pattern	-
Information Search Process	Kuhlthau, 1991 [33]	Information Seeking	Yes	Initiation, Selection, Exploration, Formulation, Collection, Presentation	Students search for information as part of the writing process
Information Foraging Theory	Pirolli and Card, 1995 [44]	HCI	No	- Information scent	-
Behavioral Model based on Information Seeking Patterns	Ellis and Haugan, 1997 [15]	Information Seeking	Yes, but not sequential	Surveying, Chaining, Monitoring, Browsing, Distinguishing, Filtering, Extracting, Ending	Engineers and research scientists in an industrial environment
Information Seeking Process	Marchionini, 1997 [39]	Information Seeking	Yes	Recognize and accept an information problem, Define and understand the problem, Choose a search system, Formulate a query, Execute search, Examine results, Extract information, Reflect/iterate/stop	-
Model of Information Behavior	Wilson, 1997 [63]	Information Behavior	Yes	Context of information need, Activating mechanism, Intervening variables, Activating mechanism, Information-seeking behavior, Information processing and use	Draw upon research decision-making, psychology, innovation, health communication, and consumer research
Process model of information searching activities and knowledge	Sutcliffe and Ennis, 1998 [56]	Information Retrieval	Yes	Problem identification, Articulating needs, Query formulation and reformulation, Evaluating results	MEDLINE users

Model	Author	Area	Phases	Main Concepts / Phases	Informed by
sources					
Model of Online Information Use	Hughes et al., 2006 [25]	Online Information Use	Yes	Plan, Act, Record, Reflect	Observations of university students' use of online information for learning Based on previous models of information behavior, information seeking, information literacy, cross-cultural adaptation, and information use
Model of Programmer's Information-Seeking Behavior	Buckley et al., 2006 [5]	Software Engineering	Yes	Awareness of Problem, Focus Formulation, Information Collection: choose search system, formulate query, execute search, extract; Examine results, Information prompted action, Problem Solution	Programmers in industrial settings

2.2.1 Identify a Source Code Need

Information need is the recognition that a person's knowledge is inadequate to satisfy a goal that the person has [6]. Developers identify a source code need when they have a lack of source code knowledge or understanding to solve a software development problem. The identification of a source code need happens on the developer's mind and it is influenced by internal factors such as memory and external factors such as goal clarity, magnitude of risk, amount of control, professional and social norms, time and resource constrains, and so on [9]. After a developer is aware of a source code need, the developer can decide to pursue the search or postpone it for later, depending on the cost and benefit of the search.

A source code need, as any information need, is not static [2]. Initially, a source code need can be identified but not completely formulated or understood. According to Taylor's four levels of information needs [57], the source code need of these characteristics would be in visceral or conscious level. The next steps in the source code seeking process can help the developer better understand the need to the point that a developer can construct a rational statement of the need (Taylor's formalized need) or can rephrase the need in a form that could be understood by an information system (Taylor's compromised need). Due to the evolving nature of need during the seeking process, all the other stages of the model shown in Figure 1 have arrows returning to this stage.

When developers identify a lack of source code, they also form expectations of results that define the decision that they could take to choose the web resource they will use, the search strategies they will use, and the evaluation of the results.

2.2.2 Select Web Resource

Based on the source code need identified by a developer and the decision to pursue the search, the developer will first choose the source of information that will be used to satisfy the need. Different sources of information can be used such as documentation, code understood by the author, example code, colleagues, bug reports, and execution logs [31]. The Web has not been extensively studied as a source of information used by programmers to find source code. Some related studies on information seeking of developers in industrial settings [5] and in open source development [49] did not include the Web. Despite the lack of attention from research to this topic, developers and other professionals are using the Web to access useful information to perform their daily activities, and the Web is changing the way professionals obtain information. In the proposed model, we emphasize the use of the Web as a source of information, but the models also consider using some of the aforementioned information sources in parallel.

Commonly, the stage to Select Web Resource will follow the identification of a source code need. However, developers can return to this stage from any other stage in Figure 1. For example, a developer can choose another Web resource after having some difficulties in translating his/her need to the resource, after not being satisfied with the search results, or after not being able to use a suitable result. The next step after choosing a Web resource is to translate the source code need to the web resource vocabulary or interface.

2.2.3 Translate and Form Need to Web Resource

After choosing a web resource to look for source code, developers need to understand the interface of the web resource to identify what is the input that the system or resource is expecting from the user. The web resources that developers use the most to look for source code on the Web are in order of preference: general-purpose search engines such as Google or Yahoo, project hosting sites such as SourceForge, and code-specific search engines such as Krugle [59]. Most of the system in these categories support keyword-based search and some of them also support browsing as a starting point.

If a keyword-based search system is selected, the user will need to translate the source code need to the vocabulary used by the system. Generally, developers can express source code needs using natural language and programming languages, or a combination of both. However, source code results indexed by natural language rely on comments that are very scarce around source code and source code indexed by programming language elements is available only in some code-specific search engines. The semantic gap between the vocabulary used by the developer and the vocabulary used by the system to find matches makes the stage of translating and forming need to web resource very challenging.

Some of the web resources also support browsing in addition to keyword-based search. When using a browsing feature to start the search, developers explore the web resource to understand the categories used to organize the repository and select one of them to start the search for source code. The proposed model is not limited to query or keyword-based search system and it also supports browsing or other techniques to start the search.

Generally, developers will translate their needs to a web resource right after they chose the web resource. However, it is also possible that developers will do it after they do not obtain good results from the search while they are evaluating the results. It could also be the case that they reformulate the need to the system because a suitable source code result could not be integrated into the developer's code, or maybe because developers have a clearer understanding of the need after seeing some results from previous search attempts.

After developers successfully translate their needs into an expression or action that the system can understand, developers execute the search. Then, the system will return the results that will be evaluated in the next stage.

2.2.4 Evaluate Results

The web resource returns the results that match with the developer's query or interactions. Developers need to go over the results and evaluate if any of those meet their source code needs. There are many factors that influence developers' decisions: the task that needs to be solved, the expected results, the level of domain knowledge, past experiences, comments from colleagues, stress, risk, work environment, age, gender, among others. These factors will also influence the strategies that developers will use to evaluate the results including browsing (scan, observe, navigate, monitor) [15], or following information scents [44], among others.

Judgments are not static. They could change after observing some of the matches or after finding a good match. While evaluating results, developers make two types of judgments: relevant judgments and suitability judgments. Relevant judgments are made to identify promising candidates. Decisions take only few seconds and are based on little information.

Suitability judgments are made to identify if a promising candidate is appropriate to solve the task at hand. Decisions are based on project characteristics such as licenses, fellow users, functionality, and decisions involve careful cost benefit analysis.

Evaluation of results will commonly follow the translation of the need to the web resource. However, the evaluation of results can also be done after one suitable result was not successful to solve the development problem, then the developer can examine again the other alternatives offered by the web resource. It is possible also that the stage of evaluate results is the first one to be used in the model when developers are using recommendation systems that automate the stages of identifying the need, select resource, and translate the need to the web resource.

After developers find a set of relevant and suitable results, they will proceed to use them to address the source code need and solve the task that motivated the seeking process.

2.2.5 Use Suitable Results

Developers will use the suitable source code to address the problem that motivated the source code need. Depending on the task they are working on, they could use the source code in different ways, including:

- Copy and paste the source code, and try to compile or run
- Modify source code to fix bugs or customize to particular need
- Adapt source code before understanding: learning by doing
- Download library and integrate it to the current source code
- Reflect on code to apply the same concept, get ideas, remember previous uses
- Read and learn a concept

If developers successfully use the source code to satisfy their needs, then this stage is the last one in the model and developers will be ready to identify another source code need. However, if developers are not successful, they can go back to any of the other stages in the model because they would like to try other results, or refine their query, or select another web resource, or rethink their need after having a better understanding of what is available.

2.2.6 Influential Factors

There are many factors that influence the decisions that developers make during the source code seeking process. We classified the influential factors in the following categories:

- **Demographics**. It refers to personal characteristics of developers, such as their age, cultural background, sex, academic background, among others that can influence in the search process. This influential factor was included as an intervening variable in Wilson's model of Information Behavior [63].

- **Domain knowledge**. It refers to the knowledge that developers have about the domain of the problem they want to solve. The level of domain knowledge largely influences the seeking process, especially how developers translate their needs to Web resources and also how they evaluate results. Marchionini [39] included domain knowledge as one of the influential factors in his information seeking model. Sutcliffe and Ennis [56] suggested that not only domain knowledge is influential on the search process, but also knowledge about how to use of software systems, awareness of information resources available, and knowledge of searching strategies.

- **Environmental**. It refers to the constraints imposed by the environment, such as the time allotted to complete certain job, the geographic location of the searcher, or the organizational culture of a company. This influential factor was included as an intervening variable in Wilson's model of Information Behavior [63].

- **Emotions**. It refers to feelings that could influence developers, such as frustration for not finding what they are looking for, uncertainty for lack of knowledge on certain area, among others. This influential factor was included as an intervening variable in Wilson's model of Information Behavior [63]. Also, Kuhlthau [33] studied the feelings that searchers have in each stage of the search process. These feelings include uncertainty, optimism, confusion, frustration, doubt, clarity, sense of direction, confidence, relief, satisfaction, and disappointment.

- **Expectations**. It refers to the results that developers are expecting to find to solve a software development problem. This factor will influence how they will evaluate the source code results. The influence of the outcome or expectation was also emphasized in the model of information seeking process proposed by Marchionini [39].

- **Interpersonal/social**. It refers to influences from colleagues, friends, or other people close to the developers. For example, a colleague can recommend a specific software component or a Web resource to use as a starting point. This influential factor was included as an intervening variable in Wilson's model of Information Behavior [63].

- **Memory/past experience**. It refers to the influence that developers' previous experiences searching for source code on the Web could have on their decisions. For example, developers can select terms that were successful in previous search experiences, or some Web resources could be used based on previous good experiences. Memory and past experience is an influential factor when people look for information. The consumer behavior field [53] has largely studied its influence. Also Sutcliffe and Ennis [56] reported that long-term memory can influence how developers articulate their needs.

- **Task**. It refers to the characteristics of the software development problem that developers are trying to solve. This includes, its goal, scope, complexity, technical constrains, among others. Task was also considered an influential factor in the information seeking process proposed by Marchionini [39].

These influential factors play an important role in the source code seeking process because they will affect the activities, decision, and strategies used by developers. However, the analysis of how these factors affect the Model of Source Code Seeking on the Web is beyond the scope of this paper due to the fact that we are focusing on the evaluation of empirical studies and tools that support each stage of our model.

2.2.7   Stage Mapping of Proposed Model and Influential Models

We analyzed how the stages of our proposed Model of Source Code Seeking on the Web map the stages of the influential models. In this analysis, we included models from Table 1 that have stages. The results of our analysis are shown in Table 2. There are some stages of the influential models that do not match with our stages. Those unmapped stages are shown in the last row of Table 2. Next, we explain the mapping between each influential model and our model.

The mapping between Kuhthau's model and our model shown in Table 2 is challenging because the behavior being modeled in that case is the seeking behavior of students working on a writing assignment. Initiation and Presentation match with our stages of Identify source code need and Use suitable results respectively. We match the Selection stage with our Selection of Web resource. These two stages have different goals: select a topic in one case and select a web resource in the other. However, they are similar in that after the selection is done, the user is ready to begin with the search. The stages of Exploration, Formulation, and Collection present an evolving search and evaluation of results for different levels of understanding of the information need. These three stages map with our two stages of Translate need to Web resource and evaluate results. Kuhlthau's model emphasized the influence of emotions during the seeking process, which motivated us to include emotions as one of the influential factors discussed in 2.2.6.

Ellis proposed eight categories to describe the information seeking patterns of engineers and research scientists in an industrial environment: Surveying that includes activities to obtain an overview of the literature within a new subject field, or to locate key people operating in the field; Chaining that involves following chains of different forms of referential connections between sources to identify new sources of information; Monitoring that involves maintaining awareness of developments and technologies in a field by following some sources of information, Browsing that is used to scan all the publications to find something of particular interest; Distinguishing that include activities where information sources are ranked according to the relevance of the user perspectives, Filtering that use certain criteria and mechanisms to make the information relevant and precise such as the use of keywords searches. Extracting that involves working through sources to locate material of interest; and Ending that finishes the process of seeking.

Ellis' categories are not stages that occur one after the other as in Kuhlthau or Marchionini's models, but instead patterns of behavior that are present during information seeking activities. We mapped these patterns to the different stages where they could be used in our model. Table 2 shows this mapping. None of the patterns are related with two of our stages: Identify source code need and Use suitable results. Similarly, two patterns, Monitoring and Ending, did not fit with any of our stages. Although the Surveying pattern was observed when researchers were conducting some kind of literature research, this pattern could be also observed when developers need to select a web resource to start the search. During this selection, developers could use informal personal contacts and also computerized retrospective searches as was mentioned in the observed pattern to identify a web source that could be used as a starting point for the search. Filtering is a pattern observed when developers translate their need to a Web resource, commonly using keyword-based searches and also interacting with the system. Chaining, Browsing, Distinguishing, and Extracting are all present when developers evaluate the results to find a relevant and suitable one.

Marchionini's model of the information-seeking process in electronic environments is very similar to our model and most of their eight stages fit nicely into our stages. There are two pairs of Marchionini's stages that are subsumed into two stages in our model. The Recognize and accept an information problem stage and the Define and understand the problem stage are both included in our Identify source code need stage. We preferred to have these two activities in one stage because both of then are related with the information need. Similarly, the Formulate a query stage and Execute search stage have been included in our Translate and form a need to a Web resource stage. However, our stage is not limited to formulate queries to search systems and it also includes other ways to interact with the system. The influence of Marchionini can be seen in all the stages of our model.

Wilson's model of information behavior is based on research from different fields including decision-making, psychology, innovation, health communication, and consumer research. The model does not intent to describe a set of information seeking activities, but instead it intents to be a methodology that suggests theories to explain human behavior when people look for information. For example, the model suggests using risk/reward theory to explain users' decisions to choose sources of information. The emphasis of this model is on the 'intervening variables' such as demographic and environmental characteristics that influence human information behavior on a supportive or preventive way. We discussed these influential factors in 2.2.6. We identify three main phases related with the information seeking activities in this model: Information need, Information-seeking behavior, and Information processing and use. The first and third phases match with our stages of Identify source code need and User suitable results respectively. The Information-seeking behavior phase maps with the other three stages of our model.

Sutcliffe presents the process model of information searching activities and knowledge sources from an information retrieval perspective. The process model includes four activities that are composed of strategies, and four knowledge sources. The activities are Problem identification, Articulating needs, Query formulation and reformulation, and Evaluating results. The knowledge sources include knowledge of a specific domain, knowledge of the facilities available by a particular system, knowledge of different searchable databases and their properties, and knowledge of searching strategies. The activities of this model are mapped to the stages of our model in Table 2. Our stages of Select web resource and Use suitable results do not have a mapping with Sutcliffe's activities. Our stage of Identify source code need maps with two activities: Problem identification and Articulating needs. The Articulating needs activity was challenging to map to either Identify source code need or Translate a need to Web resource because it involves expressing the need as concepts or high level semantics that will be refined to terms to be used in queries. This activity involves a better understanding of the needs, an understanding of the system to be used, and the search terms to be used in a system. However, given the fact that this activity mainly causes the refinement of concepts and information needs, it has been mapped with our Identify source code need stage. Finally, the activities of Query formulation and reformulation, and Evaluating results fit nicely in our stages of Translate need to web resource and Evaluate results, respectively.

Hughes' reflective online information use model aims to have a better understanding of information use for learning. This model represents online information use as a holistic experience that involves information seeking, knowledge construction, and creative applications. This model has four stages phases: Plan, Act, Record, and Reflect. In the Plan phase, users investigate available resources and plan strategies to effectively use resources. This phase maps to our stages of Identify source code need and select web resource because it involves analyzing the problem and also identifying search tools. The Act phase maps with our stages of Translate need to web resource and Evaluate results because it involves executing the search plan using the selected strategies. Our stage of Use suitable results is related to the phases of Record and Reflect. Record involves activities such as book marking, saving, emailing, and printing retrieved information and Reflect involves using critical analysis of retrieved information to build up knowledge. In code search, the use of the retrieved source code could involve copy and paste of the source code (record) and integration into the local source code (reflect). The main influence of Hughes model in our model is the incorporation of the Use suitable source code stage and the concept of information use as a continuous during the seeking process. A later model [24], that includes responses (behavioral, cognitive, and affective aspects) and influences (cultural and linguistic aspects) per each phase, emphasizes that all these different aspects can impact information use in different levels.

Buckley proposes an information-seeking model for programmers involved in software maintenance. This model is unique in that it is based on direct observation of programmers working on maintenance tasks in industrial settings. However, this study did not include the Web as an information source for programmers. The emphasis of this model is on its iterative and problem oriented nature, and its characterization of developers' activities on phases and stages. The model has two phases. The Problem-oriented phase has two stages: Awareness of the problem and Focus formulation. The Solution-oriented phase has three stages: Information collection, Examine results, and Information prompted action. Information collection has four sub-stages: Choose search system, Formulate query, Execute search, and Extract. One last stage of Problem solution is also considered as the ended action. We will map the stages and sub-stages, when present, to our model. The first two stages that belong to the first phase match with our stage of Identify source code need. The sub-stages of Choose search system, Formulate query, Execute search, as well as the stage of examine results match in the same way Marchionini's phases match with our model since these stages were inspired from Marchionini's model. The only sub-stage from Buckley's model that does not match nicely with our model is Extract. For Buckley, the Extract sub-stage happens when the information seeker extracts information from information sources. We consider the extraction happens not only during the evaluation of results, but also when using the suitable results. For that reason, we included Extraction in both of our stages. We assume that the problem solution satisfactory or not occurs while using the results. For that reason we mapped Problem solution to our Use suitable results stage. The stage of Information prompted action does not match with any of our stages. This stage involves feeds back into further information-seeking activities. In our model, we do not include this action as an stage because we assume it happens at any stage in our model while the information seeker understands better his/her information need and knows what is available.

Table 2. Mapping of influential models stages with the Source Code Seeking on the Web Model

Our Model	Kuhlthau	Ellis	Marchionini	Wilson	Sutcliffe and Ennis	Hughes et al.	Buckley et al.
Identify Source Code Need	Initiation	-	Recognize and accept an information problem	Context of information need	Problem identification	Plan	Awareness of Problem
			Define and understand the problem		Articulating needs		Focus Formulation
Select Web Resource	Selection	Surveying	Choose a search system	Information-seeking behavior	-		Choose search system
Translate and Form a Need to Web Resource	Exploration Formulation Collection	Filtering	Formulate a query		Query formulation and reformulation	Act	Formulate query
			Execute search				Execute search
Evaluate Results		Chaining, Browsing, Distinguishing, Extracting	Examine results		Evaluating results		Examine results
							Extract
Use Suitable Results	Presentation	-	Extract information	Information processing and use	-	Record	Extract
						Reflect	Problem Solution
		Monitoring, Ending	Reflect/iterate/stop				Information prompted action

2.3 Tools

We analyzed software engineering tools in the areas of code search, mining software repositories, software reuse, and program comprehension. We classified them in nine groups based on their main goal. The tools included for each group are shown in Table 3.

The first group of tools supports API example oriented code search. These tools help developers identify an appropriate API to use (SNIFF, Assieme, Mica, STeP_IN_Java), look for more information about an API (Assieme, Mica), look for examples of how to use an API (SNIFF, Assieme, Mica, MAPO, STeP_IN_Java), look for how to instantiate an object of a class type derived from another class type (PARSEWeb, Prospector), and look for experts on an API (STeP_IN_Java). In this group we also included the tools that provide developers with source code examples that support different programming tasks. XSnippet provides examples for object instantiation, Strathcona provide examples that match between the structure of the code under development and the example code repository. JSearch show examples of how to use a framework or library. Finally, XFinder locate examples based on lightweight documentation.

In the second group, we have the web-based code search engines. These tools share the goal of supporting developers to search for source code on open source code projects. Most of these tools support keyword search and some additional filters such as language and license.

In the third group we have the component retrieval tools that use Information Retrieval techniques to search for software components. The first version of Maracatu uses IR and facets, and another version of Maracatu adds folksonomy. B.A.R.T. also uses facets but adds semantic web.

In the fourth group we have the integration tools that help developers integrate an already written piece of code in the current source code been written. Jigsaw provides support to integrate one method in another method or class, while Gilligan provides support to create a reuse plan to reuse a project into another project. This group also includes transformation tools such as S^6 that generate specific methods or classes that meet users' expectations. This tool also overlaps with the Test-Driven code search tools since also support test cases as part of the input.

The fifth group has the project-hosting sites. These sites provide a source code repository for open source projects and also other features that help maintenance of projects and collaboration among open source developers. SourceForge provides support for several revision controls systems such as Subversion and CVS, while Github supports only the Git revision control system. Tigris hosts projects related with software engineering tools.

In the sixth group we classified the Test-Driven code search tools which receive a test case as an input and look for source code that matches the test case structure and passes successfully the execution of the test case. In the seventh group, we have the tools that identify reuse opportunities based on the current task of the developers. The eighth group corresponds to general-purpose search engines such as Google. In the last group we included tools that do not belong to any of the previous groups such as JIRISS that provides code search functionality in an IDE and Codetrail that provides communication between Web resources and the browser.

Table 3. Classification of Tools Based on their Main Goal

Tool Goal	Tools
API Example Oriented Code Search	Prospector [38], Strathcona [23], JSearch [52], MAPO [65], Mica [55], XSnippet [47], PARSEWeb [58], STeP_IN_Java [67], Assieme [21], XFinder [12], SNIFF [7]
Web-based Code Search Engine	Agora [48], Koders[1], SPARS-J[2] [29], Google Code Search[3], Krugle[4], Sourcerer [36], Merobase [28]
Component Retrieval	Maracatu [17], Maracatu + Folksonomy [62], B.A.R.T. [14]
Integration/Transformation	Gilligan [22], Jigsaw [10], S[6] [46]
Project-hosting Sites	SourceForge[5], Tigris[6], Github[7]
Test-driven Code Search	Extreme Harvesting [26], Code Conjurer [28], CodeGenie [35]
Reuse Opportunity Recommender	CodeBroker [66], Rascal [41]
General Purpose Search Engine	Google[8]
Others	JIRISS [45], Codetrail [19]

2.4   Empirical Studies

Developer's information needs have been observed in different settings including developers in collocated software teams [31], and developers performing maintenance activities [5, 42], but without including the Web as an information source. Due to the increase of the available source code on open source repositories and general Web pages, developers are using the Web to seek source code in this huge and diverse source code repository [27]. Some empirical studies have focused on the challenges that open source components poses for software development [8, 37]. Recent empirical studies have focus on how programmers use the Web as an information source to look for useful information to complete a software task [4, 21, 55] and to look for source code specifically [1, 51, 58]. In this paper, we will focus on all these eight empirical studies, which have been carried out with different goals and different research methods. Table 4 presents a summary of the characteristics of these empirical studies.

---

[1] http://www.koders.com/

[2] http://demo.spars.info/j/

[3] http://www.google.com/codesearch/

[4] http://www.krugle.com/

[5] http://sourceforge.net/

[6] http://www.tigris.org/

[7] https://github.com/

[8] http://www.google.com/

Table 4. Summary of Empirical Studies' Characteristics

Authors and Year	Goal	Research Methods	Subject of Study	Related Tool
Brandt et al., 2009 [4]	To understand how programmers use online resources	- Laboratory study - Analyzed queries to an online programming and examination of lexical structure, refinements, and pages visited	- 20 participants' web use was observed while building an online chat room - A month of queries from 24,293 programmers making 101,289 queries about the Adobe Flex Web app in July 2008.	-
Bajrachar ya and Lopes, 2009 [1]	To understand what users of code search engines are looking for	Topic modeling analysis of a year long usage log of Koders, a code search engine on the Web	User activity log for Koders. 10 million activities from more than 3 million users during the whole 2007 year	-
Sim et al., 2009 [51]	To evaluate the effectiveness of the search sites that software developers use	Laboratory experiment	36 subjects performed an assigned search scenario on five web sites to search for source code and judged the relevance of the 10 first hits returned	-
Chen et al., 2008 [8]	To investigate the challenges that development with OSS components poses for Chinese software companies	Survey using a structured questionnaire	47 developers from 43 small, medium, and large software companies reported on 47 completed development projects	-
Umarji et al., 2008 [59]	To understand how and why programmers search for source code on the Web	Online survey with 13 closed-ended questions and two open-ended questions	69 participants contributed 58 anecdotes about how they search for source code on the Web	-

Authors and Year	Goal	Research Methods	Subject of Study	Related Tool
Hoffmann et al., 2007 [21]	To better understand what developers are searching for on the Web	Analysis of query logs and click-through data	Query logs submitted to the MSN search engine from May 2006. 15 millions queries and 339 sessions on Java programming	Assieme
Stylos and Myers, 2006 [55]	To understand how programmers used Web resources to support their programming	Observed three small programming projects in Java and a collection of screen-captures of Java programmers	The projects involved creating a new GUI Java app, creating an Eclipse plug-in, and modifying an unfamiliar open source app	Mica
Madanmohan and De', 2004 [37]	To understand the practices that companies use when they incorporate open source components.	Structured interviews with project developers in large and medium enterprises in the US and India.	16 developers from 12 companies in the US and India who worked on 13 small projects and of short duration	-

Chapter 3: Identifying a Source Code Need

Commonly, the starting point of the source code seeking on the Web is when developers identify that they need to find source code to solve a software development problem. In this section, we examine empirical studies that characterize the motivations that developers have to look for source code on the Web and the search targets. We also analyze the tools to determine the support they give to identify a source code need.

3.1   Empirical Results

We are interested in understanding why developers seek source code on the Web, the motivation, and what developers expect to find on the Web, the search target. Some empirical studies report on both the motivation and search target [4, 51, 55, 59] but some only on the target [1, 21]. An understanding of both, the motivation and the target will help us identify the types of source code needs that developers have.

We analyzed the different motivations and search targets reported by empirical studies. Based on this analysis we observed that developers are looking for source code for mainly seven reasons: to reuse source code as-is, to find examples of usage for GUI widgets or API/libraries, to remember syntactic details or frequently used functionality, to find examples to clarify how to implement functionality in a specific language or how to implement an algorithm or data structure, to learn unfamiliar concepts, to fix a bug, and to get ideas to implement a new system. Table 5 lists these source code needs and search targets. There are other needs that were identified in our analysis but were not included because they correspond to a set of the ones listed here. For example, looking for information to complete a programming task includes most of the needs in Table 5. We also did not include the needs that did not have a motivation associated. For example, Bajracharya and Lopes [1] identified topics in a source code search engine log such as framework, application, Java/JDK APIs, but the motivation for the search was not discussed.

For each type of source code need, we can identify the search target or the expected results of the search. The specific need and expected use will determine what the developer expects to find. Similar needs can have different search targets. For example consider the needs associated with APIs, if a developer is looking for an API or library to reuse as-is, he/she will expect to find the associated component and download it. However, if the developer needs to know how to use it, he will look at tutorials or code snippets with examples. Similarly, the same search target can be used to satisfy different needs. For example, a system can be reused to serve as a starting point for an implementation or can be used to get some ideas for implementation.

The list does not intent to be a complete inventory of all the needs that developers have, but a classification of the needs reported by empirical studies. Further empirical studies could be helpful to identify other source code needs that could arise outside laboratory settings.

We included in this summary the needs related to source code. However, sometimes developers do not start the search process looking specifically for source code even thought it satisfies their needs at the end. For example, if developers need to learn a new concept, they look for tutorials or other sources, but when they find source code that could be directly tested to better understand the concept, they will use it, even without fully understanding the concept in some cases. Similarly, sometimes developers are looking for components to reuse as-is, but if they are not successful finding them, they will change the target to examples or other useful information.

3.2   Tools

We analyzed the tools presented in section 2.3 to determine how they support developers to identify a source code need. We observed that few tools (only four out of 35 tools) support developers with an automatic identification of needs and suggest reuse opportunities to them. Automatically identifying user's needs is a challenging problem to solve and requires some knowledge about the user and its context, which is not commonly available on the Web. We consider that the research community should further explore these challenges and investigate how to help developers envision or identify a reuse opportunity.

Most of the tools that support developers seeking source code to reuse, assume that the developer is able to identify an opportunity to reuse and is willing to initiate the seeking process. There are few tools that proactively suggest reuse opportunities using the techniques of recommendations agents and test-driven search, as shown in Table 6. Independently of the used technique, these tools show recommendations to developers in a non-intrusive way.

Table 5. Source Code Needs and Search Targets

Need		Target
Targeted Reuse	A wrapper	A wrapper implementation
	A parser	A parser implementation
	Small functionality/feature	Code snippets
	Data structure	Data structure implementation
	Algorithm	Algorithm implementation
	GUI widget	GUI widget component
	API/library	API/library implementation Tutorials High-level articles Sample projects with source code Forums Mailing lists API/library documentation
	A system as a starting point for an implementation	System implementation
Examples of Usage	For GUI widget	Examples of GUI widget use
	For API/library	Examples of API/library use (code snippets or complete programs) API/library documentation
Reminder	For syntactic programming language details	Code snippets
	For routinely-used functionality	Code snippets
Examples to Clarify	How to implement functionality in a specific programming language	Code snippets
	Implementation of data structure	Data structure implementation to be used as example
	Implementation of algorithm	Algorithm implementation to be used as example
Conceptual Learning		Tutorials How to articles Code snippets in tutorials to be used as examples
Bug Fix		Code snippets Patch Any helpful information to fix the bug
Ideas to Implement a New System		System implementation

Recommendation Agents

We identified three tools in this category: CodeBroker, Rascal, and Koder's plug in. CodeBroker [66] and Rascal [41] automatically identify reuse opportunities. Both tools use agents and suggest a set of methods that a developer should consider to invoke in the task at hand without leaving their development environment. Although these tools are similar in their goal, they are different in their emphasis. CodeBroker emphasizes the cognitive and social aspects of recommendations while Rascal emphasize the accuracy of the algorithms used to recommend.

In both cases the recommendations are relevant to the task the developer is currently working on, but CodeBroker also makes recommendations based on the background knowledge of an individual developer. More precisely, Rascal recommends methods based on previous developers solutions learned by the agent from mining source code repositories. CodeBroker makes recommendations based on the current source code, the interaction history between a developer and the tool (discourse model), and the developer's knowledge about the reuse repository (user model).

Rascal and CodeBroker have some limitations. Rascal is limited in that it does not use historical developer information. CodeBroker is limited in that it relies on documentation for components in the form of Javadoc for matching and also relies on developers documenting their code. The quality of the documentation of comments and components will affect its performance.

Another tool that seems to match in the recommendation agents' category is the Koder's plug in. Unfortunately, the internals of this plug-ins are not publicly available due to the fact that it is part of a commercial product. Thus, we consider that this tool falls into this category due to the behavior we observed when we tried the tool. Koders has plug-ins for Eclipse and Microsoft Visual Studio that use the SmartSearch™ technology to recommend potential opportunities for source code reuse. The plug-in performs a search to the Koders repository when the user finishes writing a method signature. The search is done in the background and the tool shows the number of source code files that contain a match for the signature. If the user clicks on the recommendations, a browser will be opened showing the result web page from Koders.

Test-driven Code Search

Code Conjurer [28] identifies reuse opportunities when developers execute unit test cases. It suggests a set of classes that pass the test cases and could be reused to implement the functionality related to the test case. This approach fits with the practice of test-driven development [3] where developers write unit test cases first and then they write enough source code to make the test cases pass. Code Conjurer makes recommendations based on the matching of components in the repository with the test case signature and only shows the user the components that successfully pass the test cases. This approach cannot return GUI classes (30% in the repository) because these classes need user interaction for test execution.

This approach is useful to predict reuse opportunities when developers create test first. However, in the case that a more traditional software process is used, and developers write test cases after implementation, the recommendation will be too late. The tool also supports the later approach, where developers design before implementing, by monitoring the changes of the UML representation of a component and suggesting components that match with the design.

Table 6. Tool Support to Identify Source Code Need

Approach	Tools
Recommendation Agents	CodeBroker, Rascal, Koders plug in
Test-driven Code Search	Code Conjurer

3.3 Summary

Empirical studies have identified that developers seek source code on the Web to satisfy seven source code needs: to reuse source code as-is, to find examples of usage for GUI widgets or API/libraries, to remember syntactic details or frequently used functionality, to find examples to clarify how to implement functionality in a specific language or how to implement an algorithm or data structure, to learn unfamiliar concepts, to fix a bug, and to get ideas to implement a new system. The search target that developers are looking for depends directly on the need and could include code snippets, API/ library implementation, tutorials, high-level articles, forums, mailing lists, API/library documentation, system implementation, among others.

Some empirical studies reported only on the search targets [1, 21] and not on the motivation that developers have to look for source code on the Web. The studies that reported both motivation and target were done using laboratory settings [51, 55], a questionnaire [8, 59], and a combination of log analysis and laboratory experiment [4]. There is need for empirical studies that observe developers in industrial settings looking for source code to identify their motivation to look for source code on the Web and the search target they expect to find.

Most of the tools require users to identify the source code need before using the tools and only few tools, only four out of 35 tools, help developers automatically identify a source code need. The tools that provide support to identify a source code need capture the context and user information from an IDE in order to make recommendations. It remains a challenge to integrate the context information from an IDE with the available information on the Web. Some approaches have been proposed to integrate these two worlds using techniques such as building an integration mechanism between IDE and the Firefox browser as done by Mica. Another technique uses plug-ins to capture the context in the IDE and send queries to Web applications as in the case of Koders and its plug-in. Further research is needed to investigate ways to take advantage of both the IDE and the Web to identify source code needs and make recommendations.

Chapter 4: Selecting a Web Resource

After a developer has identified a source code need and has decided to satisfy it using the Web, the developer, affected by different task and human factors, chooses a Web resource to start the seeking process. Here we identify the Web resources used by developers for the different source code needs based on the empirical studies done to developers. We also present the tools that support developers on choosing a Web resource to seek for source code.

4.1   Empirical Results

Empirical studies of developers using the Web have identified mainly five types of Web resources that are used as starting point for the source code seeking process. The selection of one of these types of resources will depend on the source code need, the expected results, and also on some human factors.

All the analyzed empirical studies reported on what are the Web resources that are frequently used by developers who look for source code. We classified these resources in five categories: general-purpose search engine, project hosting site, code search engine, official documentation, and others. Table 7 shows the Web resources reported and the ranking assigned for each empirical study, where (1) represents the most used Web resource, (2) the second most used Web Resource, and so on. Some empirical studies reported on what Web resources are used depending on the source code needs. This information is shown in Table 8.

Table 7. Ranking of Web Resources Used to Start the Source Code Seeking Process

Study	General-Purpose Search Engine	Project Hosting Site	Code Search Engine	Official Documentation	Others
Brandt et al. Stylos and Myers	(1)	-	-	(2)	
Bajracharya and Lopes	-	-	(1)	-	
Umarji et al. Sim et al.	(1)	(2)	(3)	-	
Hoffman et al.	(1)	-	-	-	
Chen et al.	(1)	(2)	-	-	
Madanmohan and De'	(1)	-	-	-	(2) Freshmeat (3) Corporate Portal

Seven out of eight empirical studies reported that a general-purpose search engine, such as Google or Yahoo!, is the most used Web Resource to look for source code on the Web. According to a web survey by Umarji et al. and Sim et al. [51, 59], 87% of respondents indicated that they use general-purpose search engines as an information source to search for source code. One of the main advantages of this type of Web resource is that it indexes a great variety of documents, and not only source code repositories, that can contain information related with source code such as tutorials, forums, blogs, etc. This huge index also allows users to find correct answers even when they use incorrect terminology [55]. A general-purpose search engine is very useful when developers do not know exactly what they are looking for. The results from a search in a system like Google, can help developers refine his/her need based on what is available. Due to these reasons, developers can use this type of Web sites to start the seeking process for any type of source code needs as shown in Table 8. On the other hand, one of the disadvantages of general-purpose search engines is that source code is indexed as text and it does not take advantage of its structure. Another disadvantage pointed by Stylos and Myers [55] is that this type of Web resource does not show results to emphasize source code or characteristics of it that could help developers make decisions about the relevance of a result in the result page.

Three empirical studies indicated that project-hosting sites are the second most used Web resources to look for source code on the Web. Umarji et al. and Sim et al. reported that 54% of participants use this type of Web resource [51, 59]. Some examples of project-hosting sites are GitHub, SourceForge, and Tigris.org. The main goal of project-hosting sites is to serve as a repository to open source software developers and to make open source projects available to users. The basic functionality they offer to developers looking for open source projects is a keyword search based on the name of the project and its description, and also browsing projects by category. These sites are also including other services to allow for more collaboration and awareness between developers/users such as news feed, followers for projects and developers, and more detailed statistics per project, among others features that could help users select an open source project. Developers use this Web resource when their main goal is to reuse subsystems (wrappers, parsers, data structure, algorithms, API, frameworks) or systems, to know what API/library is appropriate, to clarify the implementation of algorithms or data structures, to fix a bug (look for a patch), or to get ideas for a new system. It is less commonly used when developers are looking for just snippets of source code to learn, remember, clarify how to implement functionality in a specific programming language, or know how to use a library.

Table 8. Web Resources Used to Start the Seeking Process by Type of Source Code Need

Need		Web Resource to Start Seeking
Targeted Reuse	A wrapper	General-purpose Search Engine Project hosting sites Source code search engines
	A parser	
	Small functionality/feature	
	Data structure	
	Algorithm	
	GUI widget	
	API/library	
	A system as a starting point for an implementation	
Examples of Usage	For GUI widget	General-Purpose Search Engine
	For API/library	General-Purpose Search Engine JDK's Javadoc documentation
Reminder	For syntactic programming language details	Sometimes General-Purpose Search Engine Official language documentation page
	For routinely-used functionality	
Examples to Clarify	How to implement functionality in a specific programming language	Often General-Purpose Search Engine
	Implementation of data structure	General-purpose Search Engine Project hosting sites Source code search engines
	Implementation of algorithm	
Conceptual Learning		Almost always General-Purpose Search Engine
Bug Fix		General-purpose Search Engine Project hosting sites Mailing lists Forums
Ideas to Implement a New System		General-purpose Search Engine Project hosting sites Source code search engines

Umarji et al. and Sim et al. reported that source code search engines were used by 16% of developers when they were looking for source code [51, 59]. Koders, Krugle, Google Code Search, and Sourcerer are some examples of this web resource. These source code search engines create their indexes based on the source code itself. This is good because developers can search for specific keywords and name of methods, but at the same time is challenging when developers use only natural language in their queries, which only matches with comments in the source code. This Web resource can be useful to find code snippets to satisfy different types of source code needs, but users who already know to a high level of specificity about what to look for will benefit more from these resources [1].

Brandt et al. and Stylos and Myers reported that official documentation, such as JDK's Javadoc, was used as a starting point to look for source code on the Web. This resource is used mainly to know how to use an API/library [55] or to remember syntactic programming language details or functionality already used [4] as seen in Table 8. Brandt et al. [4] observed that sometimes developers keep open a browser tab with the website of official documentation and they will browse directly there when they need to remember about syntactic details.

Madanmohan and De' reported two other Web resources also used by developers. These include Freshmeat and corporate portals. The first one maintains an index of Unix and cross-platform software. It also offers news on new releases and a variety of original content on technical, political, and social aspects of software and programming. Corporate portals are internal applications where employees of a company keep track of open source projects used. We would add to the list of other Web resources, forums and mailing lists, which are commonly used when developers are trying to fix a bug.

The decision on the Web resource to use depends not only on the source code need, as mentioned before, but also on the seeker's domain knowledge, memory/past experience with systems, and interpersonal/social interactions. Domain knowledge is acquired by reading software related articles, news, and checking mailing lists that could have similar questions to the ones the seeker wants to solve, among others. All these sources can provide ideas for starting points of a code search. In addition, Web resources to be used can also be suggested by interpersonal and social interactions. Developers can receive recommendations on an active or passive way. Developers can ask directly to peers about Web resources or software components they might have used in the past. It could also be in a passive way if a developer is part of a conversation where peers talk about the systems they use to look for source code or the components they reuse. It is especially valuable when other peers recommend a system based on previous experience with it. The aforementioned factors that affect the selection of an information source were identified by Sim et al. [51] as domain knowledge, references from peers, and mailing lists. We would add the memory/past experience with system and expectations to this list. Developers will try to remember what worked in the past to look for a similar component and use it again if the results were successful. Also the expectations of what developers are looking for will play an important role. For example, if developers expect to find a code snippet not a subsystem or system, they would prefer to use general-purpose search engines or code search engines instead of project-hosting sites.

Empirical studies help us understand which Web resources software developers use to satisfy their source code needs. The empirical results examined in this section give us a general idea of the types of Web resources that developers use, but further empirical studies are needed to identify which resources are used for each type of source code need in particular. This information will be helpful for tools that could recommend Web resources to use depending on the intent of the user.

4.2 Tools

In this section, we analyze the tools presented in 2.3 to determine how these tools help developers choose a Web resource to be used as a starting point to seek source code on the Web.

According to the World Wide Web Consortium (W3C), a Web resource is identified by a Uniform Resource Identifier (URI) and can be accessed using the HTTP protocol. Some examples of Web resources are Web pages, a collection of Web pages, email-messages, images, etc. Web resources can be categorized according to its content. We observed that Web resources that help developers locate source code fall in one of these three categories:

- Web Page: it consists of a Web resource with zero, one, or more embedded Web resources intended to be rendered as a single unit, and referred to by the URI of the one Web resource which is not embedded [34]. Example: The "Developing an Applet" Web Page[9].

- Web Site: a collection of interlinked Web pages, including a host page, residing at the same network location [34]. Example: "Developer Resources for Java Technology" is a Web Site whose host page is http://java.sun.com/

- Web Broker: it is a Web Site that helps users identify Web Brokers or Web Sites that can provide relevant information for a specific query. For example, in the travel domain, "Fare Compare"[10] is a Web Broker that identifies other Web Brokers such as "TravelZoo"[11] and Web Sites such as "PriceLine"[12]. "Fare Compare" and "TravelZoo" redirect the user to other travel Web Sites to see details about the airline tickets requested. Others like "PriceLine" do not redirect the user to other travel sites, but instead show information about airline tickets pricing.

Figure 3. Taxonomy of Web Resources

Figure 3 shows the taxonomy of Web resources. Programmers can choose to use Web Brokers such as Google or Web Sites such as Sourcerer as starting points for seeking source code on the Web.

We expected to find tools that help developers choose among the available Web Brokers and Web Sites. However, we did not find any tool (among the ones analyzed) that helps developers select among Web Brokers and Web Sites based on their needs. Instead, we found that tools are acting as Web Brokers to help developers select Web sites, as Web Sites to help developers select Web pages, as Wrappers of Web Brokers or Web Sites, and

---

[9] http://java.sun.com/docs/books/tutorial/deployment/applet/developingApplet.html

[10] http://www.farecompare.com/

[11] http://supersearch.travelzoo.com/

[12] http://www.priceline.com/

as Repositories, as shown in Figure 4. We identified three tools that act as Web Brokers, twelve tools that act as Web Sites, five tools that act as Wrappers of Web Resources, twelve tools that act as Repositories, and three tools that do not fall in any of these categories. This classification is shown in Table 9.

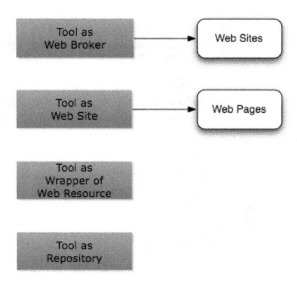

Figure 4. Tool Support Available to Select a Web Resource

4.2.1   Tool as Web Broker

Tools act as Web Brokers when they help developers find Web Sites or other Web Brokers that could satisfy developers' source code needs. We identified three tools that act as Web Brokers: Mica, Assieme, and Google. All these tools allow users to enter a set of keywords as queries and they return a set of Web Sites that are related with the query and could be appropriate to address developer's needs. These tools help developers select Web Sites but not other Web Brokers.

4.2.2   Tool as Web Site

Many of the tools are Web Sites and act as such. Similar to tools that act as Web Brokers, these tools also allow users entering a set of keywords as queries. Tools acting as Web Sites commonly return a set of Web Pages that belongs to the tool's Web Site and is related with the query indicated by the user. Some of these tools also return URLs or local Web Pages. Tools such as Koders, SPARS-J, Google Code Search, Krugle, Sourcerer, Merobase, SourceForge, Tigris, and Github are Web Sites that help developers find Web Pages in their sites that are related with the developers' source code needs. Agora and S[6] are Web Sites that after performing a search do not show web pages, but instead URLs. Agora shows

URLs of Java Beans or Corba services that match with the specified query. S^6 shows snippets of source code that pass the specified test cases and meet the indicated requirements, accompanied by the URL of the Web resource that make these snippets available. STeP_IN_Java is a Web Site that returns local (enterprise-wide) Web Pages with API Javadoc documentation.

4.2.3   Tool as Wrapper of Web Broker or Web Site

Some tools, mainly Eclipse Plug-ins, select a specific Web resource to get source code from the Web. The tool processes or filters this source code to show snippets that meet the user's requirements. These tools do not return a set of Web Sites or Web Pages, but instead a set of code snippets. For that reason, these tools do not help users select a Web resource to be used as a starting point for a search. However, developers can use these tools as a starting point to look for source code on the Web.

We identified two types of wrappers, the ones for Web Brokers and the ones for Web Sites. Extreme Harvesting is the only Wrapper of Web Broker that we identified. It uses Google to get snippets of source code. MAPO, PARSEWeb, Code Conjurer, and Code Genie are Wrappers of Web Sites. These tools obtain source code from Koders, Google Code Search, Merobase, and Sourcerer respectively. As mentioned before, they return snippets of source code to the user, except for the case of Code Conjurer that also shows the URL from where the code was obtained.

4.2.4   Tool as Repository

Tools that act as Repositories do not help developers choose a Web Resource. These tools mainly use local repositories to get source code. The local repositories are populated with source code and documentation downloaded from the Web, source code and documentation previously developed by a company or group of developers, or source code of projects that developers are currently working on their IDE workspaces. These tools return snippets of source code or documentation from their local repository. For that reason these tools do not help developers choose a Web resource to be used as a starting point of a search. In this group we found the following tools: Prospector, Strathcona, JSearch, XSnippet, XFinder, SNIFF, Maracatu, Maracatu + Folksonomy, B.A.R.T., Code Broker, Rascal, and JIRISS.

Notice that all the tools that act as Web Sites also use local repositories, but they have been considered in that group because they can be accessed though a URL and they help developers choose Web Pages. For example, Sourcerer uses a local repository populated from source code repositories such as SourceForge and it has been considered a Web Site in our classification.

4.2.5   Others

Few tools do not fall in any of the previous categories. These tools do not act as Web Brokers. They are not Web Sites or Wrappers of Web Resources, and they are not repositories either. Gilligan and Jigsaw help developers with the integration of already found source code. Thus, they do not help developers look for source code or Web Resources to find it. Codetrail uses multiple Web Resources to integrate the IDE with the Web Browser. This tool helps developers identify what are the Web Resources that are related with the source code on the IDE workspace while the developer is navigating the Web using a Web browser or saving a file in the IDE. However, the tool does not help developers identify a Web Resource that could be used as a starting point to look for source code.

Table 9. Web Resources Supported by Tools

Tool Goal	Tool Name	Tool Acts As				Tool Helps Select		
		Web Broker	Web Site	Wrapper of Web Resource	Repository	Web Site	Web Page	Other Web Resources
API Example Oriented Code Search	Prospector				♦			
	Strathcona				♦			
	JSearch				♦			
	MAPO			♦				
	Mica	♦				♦		
	XSnippet				♦			
	PARSEWeb			♦				
	STeP_IN_Java		♦					Local Javadoc
	Assieme	♦				♦		
	XFinder				♦			
	SNIFF				♦			
Web-based Code Search Engine	Agora		♦					URL
	Koders		♦				♦	
	SPARS-J		♦				♦	
	Google Code Search		♦				♦	
	Krugle		♦				♦	
	Sourcerer		♦				♦	
	Merobase		♦				♦	
Component Retrieval	Maracatu				♦			
	Maracatu + Folksonomy				♦			
	B.A.R.T.				♦			
Integration/Transformation	Gilligan							
	Jigsaw							
	S⁶		♦					URL
Project-hosting Sites	SourceForge		♦				♦	
	Tigris		♦				♦	
	Github		♦				♦	
Test-Driven	Extreme Harvesting			♦				

Tool Goal	Tool Name	Tool Acts As				Tool Helps Select		
		Web Broker	Web Site	Wrapper of Web Resource	Repository	Web Site	Web Page	Other Resources / Web Resources
Code Search	Code Conjurer			◆				URL
	CodeGenie			◆				
Reuse Opportunity Recommender	CodeBroker				◆			
	Rascal				◆			
General Purpose Search Engine	Google	◆				◆		
Others	JIRISS				◆			
	Codetrail							

4.3   Summary

All the empirical studies evaluated reported on the frequently used Web resources that developers use to look for source code on the Web. Almost all the studies agreed that the most used Web resource is a general-purpose search engine. Developers also used project-hosting sites, code search engines, and official documentation. Other Web resources also used include forums, corporate portals, and mailing lists. Empirical studies are needed to observe in practice what Web resources are used by developers for specific types of source code need and what factors affect the decision to use one Web resource over others.

All the tools that help developers choose a Web resource act as Web Brokers, Web Sites, and Wrappers of Web Resources. These tools help developers select a Web Site or a Web page inside a Web Site. Most of the tools, except Mica, Assieme, and Google, work with only one Web Site and recommend Web Pages inside that Web Site. Commonly, the recommended Web page is not used as a starting point for code seeking but instead the needed source code could be found there.

We expected to find tools that help developers choose among the available Web Brokers and Web Sites for source code seeking. For instance, we expected tools that could help developers decide if for a specific source code need is better to use Google, SourceForge, or Sourcerer, or show a comparison of results given by these tools similarly to tools for buying airline tickets such as FareCompare[13]. Tools with the mentioned characteristics will be very useful for developers but there is no one like that currently.

Chapter 5: Translate and Form Need to Web Resource

Once developers select a Web resource to help them during the source code seeking process, they need to translate their needs into the Web resource using the interface the resource provides. In this section, we examine empirical studies that identify the techniques that developers use to translate their needs and we also analyze how well tools support developers to translate and form their source code needs.

5.1   Empirical Results

Developers mainly use two strategies to translate and form a source code need to a Web resource: by query formulation and reformulation, and by browsing. Query formulation is the most used technique by developers. They generally use search terms in natural language, programming language, and a combination of both.

Six empirical studies examined how developers translate their needs to Web Resources. All these studies observed that developers use query formulation [1, 4, 21, 51, 55, 59], two observed the use of query reformulation [4, 51], and one the use of browsing [4]. These studies provide examples of queries that developers form to address many of the different types of source code needs. Table 10 shows examples of these queries by type of source code need. Based on the examples given and observation from empirical studies, we can group the queries in three categories: the ones that are expressed in natural language, the ones expressed in programming language, and the ones that use a combination of both.

---

[13] http://www.farecompare.com/

Natural language queries are common when developers are trying to learn new concepts. In that case, they will use natural language to describe the problem they need to solve and will include some terms related with the technology or programming language they plan to use. It is also common that when developers are trying to learn new concepts, they use query reformulation based on the familiar terms that they see in the result page [4]. Using query reformulation also helps developers refine their need and their expectation of what they are looking for. Bajracharya and Lopes [1] found that natural language queries are prevalent but they do not result in as much download as others. Natural language queries are also used when developers are trying to fix a bug. Some times developers will describe the bug in natural language and often they will just copy and paste the exact error. Query refinements are not common when developers are looking for a bug fix.

Programming language queries are frequently used when developers use the web as an external memory aid to remember syntactic details and functionality used repeatedly such as connecting to a database. In these cases, developers do not use much query refinement because they know exactly what they are looking for [4].

A combination of natural language and programming language is used for the rest of the source code need types that empirical studies have reported on. Based on the query examples provided, in most of the cases the natural language is a more technical language that is clear only to software developers. Keywords from programming languages are added when developers have a better knowledge about the expected result. For example, when developers already know an API and are looking for how to use some specific methods, then they will include the name of the method in the query and programming language keywords as needed [55]. An interesting combination of technical language and programming language is the one used when developers have the need to clarify how to implement functionality in a specific programming language. In that case, developers will include programming language terms in the query, but these will be from a different programming language from the one they want to obtain the clarification. This is due to the fact that developers are familiar with a concept in a programming language but do not know how to implement it in another programming language.

Browsing was used when developers were navigating through official language documentation when they wanted to know how to use API/libraries or they wanted to remember syntactic details or frequently used functions.

Table 10. Query and Query Reformulation Used by Type of Source Code Need

Need		Query	Query Reformulation
Targeted Reuse	A wrapper	e.g. "Java wrapper code for the native pcap library"	-
	A parser	e.g. "RSS feed parser"	-
	Small functionality/feature	e.g. "encode/decode URL" "convert uploaded images of all types to jpeg"	-
	Data structure	There is a close match between the vocabulary in the code and the vocabulary for describing the search e.g. "two-way hash tables," "B+ tree," "trie trees"	-
	Algorithm	There is a close match between the vocabulary in the code and the vocabulary for describing the search e.g. "binary search algorithm"	-
	GUI widget	e.g. "inserting a browser in Java Swing frame"	
	API/library	e.g. "speech processing toolkits" "library for date manipulation in Perl" "Java implementations of statistical techniques"	
	A system as a starting point for an implementation	-	-
Examples of Usage	For GUI widget	-	-
	For API/library	Queries contain API or package names, type names, or method names. Queries also contain descriptive keywords and some included a term to indicate the type of document a developer was looking for: eg. "Java doc", "tutorial", "download" When looking for examples: Queries contained terms like "example", "using", or "sample code" Browsing the list of classes in the JDK	
Reminder	For syntactic programming language details	Mostly code. e.g. "mysql_fetch_array"	Usually zero query refinements
	For routinely-used functionality	Mostly code. Browsing official documentation to find how to connect to a MySQL database	Usually zero query refinements
Examples to Clarify	How to implement functionality in a specific programming	Mix of natural language and code with cross language analogies. Queries contained more programming-language-specific term than learning ones. . Often terms were not from the correct programming language.	Few query refinements

Need		Query	Query Reformulation
	language	Programmers made language analogies Eg. "javascript timer"	
	Implementation of data structure	-	-
	Implementation of algorithm	-	-
Conceptual Learning		Natural language related to high-level task Natural-language description of a problem they were facing, often augmented with several keywords specifying technology they planned to use. "update web page without reloading php" "ajax tutorial" "examples of thread implementation in python"	Usually several. Query refinements are common often before the user clicked on any results. Refinements were driven by familiar terms seen on the query result page "ajax update php"
Bug Fix		Search for exact error or Natural language queries with the keywords from an error message or keywords based on the functionality deviation caused by a bug or defect e.g. "XML filtering Predicate Operator Called on Incompatible Functions"	Few query refinements
Ideas to Implement a New System		-	-

5.2   Tools

In this section, we analyze the tools presented in 2.3 to determine the support they provide to help developers translate their source code needs to the tools. Table 11 shows the results of our analysis. For each tool, this table indicates the user interface and the techniques supported by tools to translate the source code needs. This table includes the techniques identified in the empirical studies: query formulation, reformulation, and browsing. We also added information about the support of the tools to help developers select keywords and connectors to form the query. Some of the tools support automatic translation of needs or other techniques that have also been included in this summary table.

We found that most of the tools support query formulation, but only some of them include support to select keywords and connectors to form the query. Query reformulation was also supported by some of the tools. Most of the tools that do not support query formulation, automatically translate the source code need based on the current programming task that developers are working on an IDE. Few tools support browsing or other ways to specifying source code needs.

5.2.1   Support for Query Formulation and Reformulation

Twenty-three tools allow developers to enter a query of keywords to specify their needs. These keywords are commonly typed in an input box in the graphical interface, except for JSearch that takes queries from source code comments. Generally, developers need to select keywords and connectors to include in the query without any help from the tool. However, ten of the tools, Agora, Koders, Google Code Search, Krugle, Sourcerer, Merobase, Maracatu, Maracatu + Folksonomy, Github, and JIRISS, offer some help to include keywords. These tools help developers identify keywords by showing related GUI elements such as a dropdown list for all the supported languages or providing special query indicators such as "lang:" for languages. Most of these tools help developers include information related with the desired language of the code snippet in the query. Some tools also remind the user to include information about the component type (Java Bean, Corba, EJB, WebService), the domain (manufacturing, finance), the platform (J2EE, J2ME), and tags. Even a fragment of source code could be used to form a query as done by JIRISS.

Five of these twenty-three tools, JSearch, Agora, Google Code Search, Sourcerer, and Google, help developers connect the keywords in the query using connectors. The possible connectors to be used are not showed in the GUI, but instead these should be used directly in the query. These tools allow developers to use Boolean algebra and/or regular expressions.

Six of these twenty-three tools, Mica, STeP_IN_Java, Google Code Search, B.A.R.T., Google, and JIRISS, show suggestions to help users refine their queries. These suggestions are made after the first query has been run and are based on the initial query. In addition to those six tools, CodeBroker that does not support query input but instead forms a need automatically, also offers the user the option of reformulating the query automatically formed by the tool. All these tools offer support for query reformulation using different techniques including: spelling correction; listing domain terms, software vocabulary, or method and class names related to the query; using search by refinement to personalize the search by limiting the scope to a specified package or class; or retrieval by reformulation.

5.2.2 Automatic Translation of Needs

Some tools do not require the user to enter a query. These tools either will infer a source code need based on developers' actions or they will translate the need automatically based on the user context after the user requests to initiate the search. The tools that infer a source code need are Koder's Plug-in, Code Conjurer, CodeBroker, and Rascal. These tools help developers identify source code needs and were discussed in detail in section 3.3.

The tools that translate automatically user's needs upon the user's request are Prospector, Strathcona, XSnippet, XFinder, and Codetrail. The first four tools look for examples of source code when the user requests it. The requirements of the needed examples are formed automatically by the tool based on the context of the current task that the developer is working on. The context is taken from the position of the cursor and the structure of source code for Prospector, Strathcona, and XSnippet. For XFinder, the context is taken from a step in the Mismar guide.

Finally, Codetrail automatically translate user's needs when the user is navigating web pages in a browser or saving source code in an IDE. When a developer is visiting web pages in a Web browser, the tool detects if the Javadoc or documentation Web page is relevant to source code currently loaded in the IDE. When developers save a file, the tool detects the newly written source code and it identifies if that source code is similar to the one found in any of the recently visited web pages.

5.2.3 Browsing

Few of the analyzed tools, only four, provide developers the option of indicating their needs by browsing the organization of the source code. SPARS-J allows users browsing packages, Maracatu + Folksonomy allows users browsing tags, and SourceForge and Tigris support browsing by project categories. These four tools offer the browsing option in addition to query formulation.

5.2.4 Others

We found four tools that allow users to express their needs in other ways different from queries and browsing. Extreme Harvesting and Code Genie allow the user to express their needs as test cases. Code Conjurer also uses test cases, but the tool infers the need when test cases are saved. S6 supports query formulation, but it also allows users to indicate their need using class or method signature, test cases, contracts (pre condition and post condition), and security constraints.

Table 11. Techniques Supported by Tools to Translate Source Code Needs

Tool Goal	Tool Name	User Interface	Support for Query Formulation			Reformulation	Browsing	Automatic Translation	Others
			Query Input	Select Keywords	Select Connectors				
API Example Oriented Code Search	Prospector	Eclipse Plug-in						◆	
	Strathcona	Eclipse Plug-in						◆	
	JSearch	Eclipse Plug-in Web Application	◆		◆				
	MAPO	Unknown	◆						
	Mica	Web Application	◆			◆			
	XSnippet	Eclipse Plug-in						◆	
	PARSEWeb	Eclipse Plug-in	◆						
	STeP_IN_Java	Web Application	◆			◆			
	Assieme	Web Application	◆						
	XFinder	Eclipse Plug-in extending Mismar						◆	
	SNIFF	Eclipse Plug-in	◆						
Web-based Code Search Engine	Agora	Web Application	◆	◆	◆				
	Koders	Web Application Eclipse and Visual Studio Plug-in	◆	◆				◆	
	SPARS-J	Web Application	◆				◆		
	Google Code Search	Web Application	◆	◆	◆	◆			
	Krugle	Web	◆	◆					

Tool Goal	Tool Name	User Interface	Support for Query Formulation Query Input	Select Keywords	Select Connectors	Reformulation	Browsing	Automatic Translation	Others
		Application Eclipse Plug-in							
	Sourcerer	Web Application	◆	◆	◆				
	Merobase	Web Application	◆	◆					
Component Retrieval	Maracatu	Eclipse Plug-in	◆	◆					
	Maracatu + Folksonomy	Eclipse Plug-in	◆	◆			◆		
	B.A.R.T.	Eclipse Plug-in	◆			◆			
Integration/Transformation	Gilligan	Eclipse Plug-in							
	Jigsaw	Eclipse Plug-in							
	S^6	Web Application	◆						Classes or method signature, test cases, contracts, and security constraints
Project-hosting Sites	SourceForge	Web Application	◆				◆		
	Tigris	Web Application	◆				◆		
	Github	Web Application	◆	◆					
Test-Driven Code Search	Extreme Harvesting	Unknown							Signature of the desired component and

Tool Goal	Tool Name	User Interface	Support for Query Formulation			Reformulation	Browsing	Automatic Translation	Others
			Query Input	Select Keywords	Select Connectors				
									test cases
	Code Conjurer	Eclipse Plug-in						♦	Test case signature or a UML diagram
	CodeGenie	Eclipse Plug-in							Test case
Reuse Opportunity Recommender	CodeBroker	Display in Emacs				♦		♦	
	Rascal	Eclipse Plug-in						♦	
General Purpose Search Engine	Google	Web Application	♦		♦	♦			
Others	JIRISS	Eclipse Plug-in	♦	♦		♦			
	Codetrail	Eclipse Plug-in Firefox Plug-in						♦	

5.2.5 Summary

Empirical studies identified that developers use query formulation/reformulation and a little bit of browsing to translate their source code needs to Web resources. Queries are formulated differently depending on the developers' source code needs. These are sometimes written in natural language, others in programming languages, and often using a combination of both. After analyzing the data reported by empirical studies, we could not answer the following question: why were other techniques such as query by example not observed? Is it because tools do not support other strategies or is it because people do not use them? Further empirical studies are needed to understand other ways that developers can interact with Web resources beyond a box for keywords and observe if other techniques will be more beneficial for developers and their different types of source code needs.

The analysis of tools revealed that almost all the tools support query formulation. That means that users have to form their own query. However, some tools also help developers select keywords and connectors to form the query as well as query reformulation. Few tools support browsing and automatic translation of needs based on the context of the user.

Chapter 6: Evaluate Results

Web resources will present a list of source code results that match with the query provided by developers. Developers will evaluate the source code results using multiple criteria depending on their source code need. In this section, we examine empirical studies that report on what are the criteria developers use to select a relevant and suitable source code results that will help them solve a software development problem. We also analyze how well tools support developers to evaluate a list of source code results given by Web resources.

6.1   Empirical Results

After developers translate their source code need to the Web resources, a list of results, that are assumed to be relevant for the developer's needs, is shown. Developers need to determine which of the matches returned are relevant and suitable for their development problem. In order to do the evaluation of results, developers apply some judgment strategies and criteria to choose the best match to be used. Different types of source code needs require different judgment criteria and strategies. However, few empirical studies report on the set of activities carried out to do the evaluation for each type of source code need.

We found six empirical studies that report on how developers evaluate source code results to select one option that satisfies their source code needs. Two studies report on questionnaires [8, 59], two on lab experiments [51, 55], one on a laboratory experiment and log analysis [4], and one on a field site [37]. First, we present the empirical results related to the evaluation criteria used when developers are looking for code snippets, and then the criteria used when developers are looking for open source components and projects.

6.1.1 Code Snippets

We summarized the empirical results that report on the evaluation of code snippets in Table 12. This table includes information about the judgment strategy, judgment criteria, and the time spent during a session for some source code needs. Stylos and Myers [55] reported on how developers evaluate results when they are looking for examples of how to use an API (see first row in Table 12). He found that developers often open and scan some of the results pages to look for methods or class names based on cosmetic features such as fixed width font or programming punctuation. After they find source code on the documentation pages, they check the official documentation to validate the functionality.

Brandt et al. [4] reported on how developers evaluate code snippets to remember syntactic programming language details and routinely-used functionality, to clarify how to implement functionality in a specific programming language, learn unfamiliar concepts, and fix a bug as show in rows 2-5 in Table 12. When developers try to remember, they often just view the search result snippets to find exactly what they are looking for. Occasionally, they also open at most one search result. When developers are looking for information to clarify how to implement functionality in a specific language, developers click some of the result pages and they easily recognize the source code they are looking for when they see it. When developers want to learn new concepts, they make judgments on the quality of the web page based on the prevalence of advertisement. Developers perceive that a site that has lower amount of advertisement has better quality. These judgments are made by rapidly skimming several result pages. Finally, when developers are looking for information to fix a bug they will examine the results by clicking some of the result pages. Brandt et al. also reported on the time developers spent on their session for different source code needs. Developers expend on average less than one minute when they use the Web to remember, around one minute when they are trying to clarify information, and tens of minutes when they are trying to learn a new concept.

Table 12. Evaluation of Results by Type of Source Code Need for Code Snippets

Need		Judgment Strategy	Judgment Criteria	Time Spent
Examples of Usage	For API/library	Open and scan some of the result pages	Look for code such as method or class names in web pages based on cosmetic features Check the official documentation to verify functionality	-
Reminder	For syntactic programming language details	Zero or one result click View only the search result snippets	Developers knew exactly what information they were looking for	Less than 1 minute
	For routinely-			

51

	used functionality			
Examples to Clarify	How to implement functionality in a specific programming language	Few result clicks	Developers can easily recognize the code once they find it	Around 1 minute
Conceptual Learning		Several result clicks Rapidly skim several result pages opened in tab browsers	Quality based on cosmetic features: prevalence of advertisement	Tens of minutes
Bug Fix		Few clicks on result pages	-	-

6.1.2   Open Source Components & Projects

Four empirical studies reported on how open source components and projects are evaluated [8, 37, 51, 59]. Table 13 shows a comparison of the criteria reported on these studies. The number that precedes some criteria indicates its ranking. For example (1) indicates that a criterion was the most used by developers who participated in the study. Chen et al. included 10 criteria in their study, but they only reported on most used criterion and the two least used. Umarji et al. and Sim et al. reported the ranking of the 5 criteria they identified. Madanmohan and De' reported seven criteria but did not include raking information of three of them.

All these four studies agreed that requirements or functionality are the most used criteria to evaluate open source software. Licensing was mentioned in all the studies, but Umarji et al. and Sim et al. reported it as the second more important criterion. For Madannmohan, the second more important criterion was usability or component characteristics such as flexibility and design consistency. This criterion also matches with the quality of components mentioned by Chen et al. Cost was mentioned by all the studies, two of them reported it as the third more important criterion and Chen et al. reported it as the second least important criterion. Sim et al. and Umarji et al. reported user support available as the fourth most important criterion. However, Chen et al. report it as the least important criterion. The last important criterion for Umarji et al. and Sim et al. was the level of project activity. These two last criteria match with the maintenance and support criteria mentioned by Madanmohan and De'. Finally, Madanmohan and De' indicated that familiarity, i.e. if developers have used the open source software before, is the most used criterion when resources and time are limited during the selection process.

Table 13. Evaluation Criteria for Open Source Software

Chen et al.	Umarji et al. and Sim et al.	Madanmohan and De'
(1) Requirements compliance Functionality	(1) Available functionality	(1) Functionality requirements
Open source licensing terms	(2) Licensing	Licensing
Quality of components (security, reliability, usability)		(2) Usability/Component characteristics
Architectural compliance		Architectural compatibility
Reputation of components and supplier		
Quality of documentation		
Environment or platform		
(9) Licensing price	(3) Price	(3) Costs
(10) Expected support from the open source community	(4) User support available	Maintenance and support
	(5) Level of project activity	
		(1) Familiarity

Two types of judgments have been identified when developers look for source code on the Web: relevance judgments and suitability judgments [16]. Relevance judgments are made when developers identify promising candidates. Relevance decisions are quick, in the order of seconds, and use little information. A lab experiment [51] reported that developers spent 32 seconds in average to make relevant judgments. Suitability judgments are made when developers define if a promising candidate is appropriate for the development problem at hand. Suitability decisions take more time and involve a cost benefit analysis. A lab experiment [51] reported that developers spent days or weeks to make suitable judgments. The emphasis on relevance or suitability judgments or both is different for the evaluation of results for different types of source code needs. We observe that there is a correlation between the type of judgments developers made and the certainty level of expected results as shown in Figure 5. When the expected results are close to certainty, developers mainly make relevance judgments. When the expected results are high uncertain, developers mainly make suitability judgments, and when the expected results are somewhere in-between certain, developers make both relevant and suitable judgments. Thus, when developers look for source code to remember, they usually find what they were looking for on less than one minute and make mainly relevance judgments using often only result snippets. Similarly, when developers are trying to clarify how to implement functionality in a specific programming language, they mostly make relevance judgments to find the clarification in around one minute. Developers use a combination of relevance and suitability judgments when they look for source code to know how to use an API or library and to learn. For example, in the case of developers looking for how to use an API, developers make relevance judgments based on the match of a result with the API they want to use and make suitability judgments based on how close the source code found fits with the specific problem they want to solve and with the source code developers already have. The time spent for doing the combination of relevance and suitability judgments is in the order of tens of minutes when developers want to learn a new concept. When developers look for source code to reuse as-is they have a high uncertainty on the expected results and developers will mostly make suitability judgments including matching of functionality, type of software license, social characteristics of the project, availability of a community of practice among others.

Different uncertainty levels of expected results can also be related to the exploratory search activities defined by Marchionini [40]. He defined three search activities: lookup that involves the seeker making minimal result set examination and item comparison; learn that involves the seeker spending more time scanning results, comparing, and making qualitative judgments; and investigate that involves the seeker critically assessing results for long periods of time before integrating them into his/her knowledge. Marchionini classifies the search activities of learning and investigating as exploratory search activities. For source code seeking on the Web, the search activity of lookup can be identified when developers look for source code to remember syntactic details or to clarify some implementation details. The exploratory search activity of learning can be identified when developers are looking for examples of API usage and when they want to learn unfamiliar concepts. The exploratory search activity of investigate can be identified when developers are looking for source code to reuse.

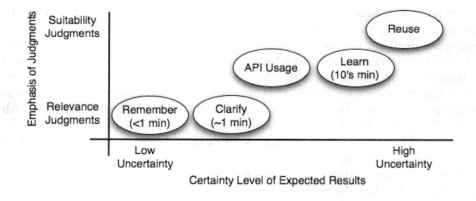

Figure 5. Correlation between Emphasis of Judgments and Certainty Level of Expected Results by Types of Source Code Needs

6.2 Tools

We analyzed the tools presented in section 2.3 to determine the support they provide the users to evaluate results returned by the tools. Commonly, tools return several elements that match with the user's query. Tools show the results in a way that will allow the user to make informed decisions about the relevance of a match in a reasonable amount of time. We observed two approaches in which tools help developers evaluate the results. First, tools rank the matches based on some criteria and show them to the user in order according to the ranking position. Second, tools show additional information for each match that could help users compare the matches and identify the more relevant and suitable for their needs. We found that all the analyzed tools that show results present them to the user using some ranking order and most of them present snippets of source code to help users evaluate the relevance based on functionality.

6.2.1 Ranking

Most of the tools included in our analysis deal with presenting source code to the users and these tools present source code results ordered by ranking. We observed that the ranking was calculated using mainly two approaches. One approach uses the structure of the source code and the other one uses document properties. Tools can use these two approaches together or separately. Table 16 shows the ranking approach for each tool and also provides additional details about the information used to rank results. Unfortunately, we did not have access to detailed ranking information for some tools. In those cases, we included the word 'unknown' in the ranking information column. We found that 16 tools use only the source code structure to rank results, 5 tools use only the source code as text, and 5 tools use both the source code structure and the source code as text to rank results. There are 3 tools that do not show ranking information, and there are 6 tools that their ranking algorithms are unknown.

6.2.1.A Ranking based on Source Code Structure

Most of the tools take advantage of more than one characteristic of the structure of the source code. We identified ten characteristics that were used by tools as shown in Table 14 ordered by the number of tools that use them. We did not include in this table the tools that use exactly the same algorithm that other tools such as Extreme Harvesting, Code Conjurer, CodeGenie, and S6. The most used characteristic was the name of classes and methods. Tools also used the dependencies among source code entities such as inheritance, interface implementation, abstract class implementation, calls, uses, and references among classes, as well as variable declaration, field access, and method invocation. Some tools also used the frequency of occurrence of a source code snippet in the repository to measure its relevance to the user.

Comments were also used to determine the matching of source code with a query, but in all the cases this characteristic was used in conjunction with other characteristics such as name of classes of dependencies. Length of the source code snippet was also considered for ranking. Commonly, the shorter the snippet the higher the ranking. In addition to the method name, in some cases the method signature was also used. The method signature provides information about the type of parameters that a method receives and also the return type.

There are four characteristics that were used only for one tool. XFinder calculates the location similarity to identify if two pieces of source code belong to the same source file, package, or project. Krugle uses repository information, such as name of files in a repository. Krugle also uses syntactic information to change the relevance of matches. For example, the tool will give higher ranking to function calls over commented text. Assieme uses the ratio of text around code snippets in web pages to determine how relevant they are.

Table 14. Source Code Characteristics Used by Tools to Rank Results

Source Code Characteristic	Tools
Name of classes, methods	JSearch, Mica, XFinder, Agora, Sourcerer, CodeBroker, Rascal, JIRISS
Dependencies	Strathcona, JSearch, XSnippet, XFinder, SPARS-J, Sourcerer
Frequency of occurrence	XSnippet, PARSEWeb, Assieme, SNIFF
Comments	JSearch, CodeBroker, JIRISS
Length	Prospector, XSnippet, PARSEWeb
Method signature	STeP_IN_Java, CodeBroker
Location	XFinder
Repository information	Krugle
Syntactic information	Krugle
Text around code snippets	Assieme

6.2.1.2 Ranking based on Document Properties

Some tools analyze some document properties to determine the relevance of results. Table 15 shows the properties of documents or algorithms used to determine ranking. Google uses PageRank to determine the relevance on a page based on the analysis of its links. This algorithm is also used by Mica to show web pages related to the user query. Assieme uses PageRank in conjunction with the ratio of text around code snippets to determine the relevance.

The component retrieval tools, Maracatu, Maracatu + Folksonomy, and B.A.R.T, do not use source code structure to calculate ranking, instead they use facets or tags related to components, and the file content and name of components.

Some tools, mainly the ones that show open source projects also take into account information about the project such as the activity level, the number of downloads, number of recent commits, number of forum posts, among other statistics. In this case, the ranking is based on project properties, more than document properties.

SourceForge uses term frequency in files along with project level information. Sourcerer also implements one of its algorithms using only term frequency. However, this algorithm did not perform as well as others that also include source code structure in the ranking algorithm [36].

Table 15. Document Properties or Algorithm Used by Tools to Rank Results

Document Properties / Algorithm	Tools
PageRank	Mica, Assieme, Google
Facets	Maracatu, B.A.R.T.
Project level information	Krugle, SourceForge
Term Frequency	SourceForge, Sourcerer
Content, File Name	B.A.R.T.
Tags	Maracatu + Folksonomy

Table 16. Ranking Criteria Supported by Tools

| Tool Goal | Tool Name | Ranking Based on | | Ranking Information |
		Source Code as Text	Source Code Structure	
API Example Oriented Code Search	Prospector		♦	It creates jungloid graphs using API signatures and sample client programs. It traverses paths from Tin to Tout where each path is a code fragment. The ranking is based on the length of the path. The shorter the path, the closer to the top ranking.
	Strathcona		♦	It matches the structural context description of the user to the code repository to find structurally similar code using four heuristics: inherits, call, uses, and references. The ranking is based on the number of heuristics that returned a candidate. Candidates returned by more heuristics are ranked as more relevant.
	JSearch		♦	It indexes the source code using: class name, class that is extended, method name, return types, comments, and import declarations. The ranking is based on the match between the query and the source code indexes using TF-IDF powered by Lucene.
	MAPO			Unknown
	Mica	♦	♦	<u>Keywords for side bar ranking</u>: It analyzes the first ten results and looks for programming words that are names of method, class, interface in the Java SDK library. The keywords that occur frequently in the search results but infrequently across the whole Web are most relevant. <u>Web pages ranking</u>: It uses the ranking given by the Google Web API.
	XSnippet		♦	It models the source code as a direct acyclic graph (DAG). It traverses the DAG and produces a set of paths that represent code snippets. The ranking is based on three heuristics: context, frequency of occurrence, and snippet length; applied in that order. Context: it uses a quantitative measure of how well the parent and type context of a code snippet matches with the parent and type context of the query. Frequency of occurrence: the higher the number of times identical code snippets are found in the repository, the higher the rank of the code

Tool Goal	Tool Name	Ranking Based on		Ranking Information
		Source Code as Text	Source Code Structure	
				snippet. Length: the lower the number of lines of code, the higher the rank of the code snippet.
	PARSEWeb		◆	It converts samples to a Direct Acyclic Graph (DAG) and extract method invocations sequences from the DAG. The ranking is based on two heuristics: frequency and length. The higher the frequency and the shorter length, the higher the rank.
	STeP_IN_Java		◆	It indexes each API method based on its name and text-based Javadoc descriptions. It computes the similarity between the user query and the documents of each method in the repository by assigning appropriate weights to terms in the document collection. Documents that best match the query have a higher ranking. The ranking is based on Code Broker's ranking.
	Assieme	◆	◆	It uses implicit references to calculate ranking for APIs and Web pages. API ranking: It uses text around code samples in Web pages and also text on Javadoc documentation pages that reference an API. It also ranks the importance of packages, classes, and members based on a logarithm of the number of times each is referenced in the sample code found by the tool. Web pages ranking: It includes Web-specific properties such as URL terms and document title among the weighting of terms related to a page. It also includes fully qualified names to external referenced objects. It sets the static score of a page to a weighted sum of its PageRank and a logarithm of the proportion of length of text around code samples with respect to the length of code samples. The tool favors short and simple code samples and helpful documentation.
	XFinder		◆	The ranking is based on the likelihood that a potential output is the right output for a Mismar step. The likelihood is calculated using four relationship types: name similarity of potential outputs, location similarity (project, package, source file), Java-to-Java

Tool Goal	Tool Name	Ranking Based on		Ranking Information
		Source Code as Text	Source Code Structure	
				relationship (calls, contains, refers to), and plug-in-to-Java relationship (relationship between Plug-ins extensions and Java classes). These four confidence ratios could be combined by: calculating the average, giving different weights based on confidence values, and favoring domain-specific relationships (Java-to-Java and plug-in-to-Java).
	SNIFF		◆	The ranking is calculated using the frequency of occurrence of code snippets in the indexed code base.
Web-based Code Search Engine	Agora		◆	Java Bean ranking: It indexes the component type (JavaBean), name (FQN of class or interface), property descriptors (bean info), methods (accessor methods), and event (set of events a bean fires). Corba ranking: It indexes the component type (CORBA), name, operation, parameter, exception, and attribute.
	Koders			Unknown
	SPARS-J		◆	Component Rank: a collection of software components is represented as a weighted directed graph. Nodes represent components and edges represent cross component usage. The usage relations that are considered are: class inheritance, interface implementation, abstract class implementation, variable declaration, instance creation, field access, and method invocation. It is similar to PageRank.
	Google Code Search			Unknown
	Krugle		◆	The ranking is based on repository information (for example: filenames) and project-level information (for example: how active it has been and how big it is). Also, syntactic information is used to boost function definitions over function calls, function calls over comment text, and so on.
	Sourcerer	◆	◆	- TF-IDF (Term frequency – inverse document frequency) on code-as-text - FQNs (Fully qualified names) of packages, classes, and methods + TF-IDF - FQNs of packages, classes, and methods + coderank + TF-IDF

Tool Goal	Tool Name	Ranking Based on		Ranking Information
		Source Code as Text	Source Code Structure	
		- Boosted FQNs of packages, classes, and methods + TF-IDF		- Boosted FQNs of packages, classes, and methods + TF-IDF
				- Boosted FQNs of packages, classes, and methods + coderank + TF-IDF
	Merobase			Unknown
Component Retrieval	Maracatu	◆		The ranking is based on the match between the query and the index that includes facets using TF-IDF powered by Lucene.
	Maracatu + Folksonomy	◆		The ranking is based on the number of times a tag appears in the database. In case folksonomy is not used, the ranking is based on the match between the query and the index that includes facets using TF-IDF powered by Lucene.
	B.A.R.T.	◆		It classifies source code (without comments) according to an infrastructure category such as security, GUI, network, using a probabilistic classifier. The infrastructure classification information along with content and file name is used to create the index structure.
Integration/Transformation	Gilligan			
	Jigsaw			
	S⁶		◆	The ranking is taken from the code search engine selected by the user among Google Code Search, Krugle, or Koders.
Project-hosting Sites	SourceForge	◆	◆	It has both relevance and ranking, but it shows the result ordered by number of downloads. Relevance: It is based in large part on the number of times that the query appears in the project documents. It uses Lucene. Ranking: It is based on Traffic (last_7_days_downloads, last_7_day_logo_hits, last_7_day_site_hits), Development (last_7_days_scm_commits, days_since_last_file_release, days_since_last_admin_login), Communication (last_7_days_tracker_entries, last_7_days_ML_posts, last_7_days_forum_posts)
	Tigris			Unknown
	Github			Unknown
Test-	Extreme	◆		It uses the ranking given by Google.

Tool Goal	Tool Name	Ranking Based on		Ranking Information
		Source Code as Text	Source Code Structure	
Driven Code Search	Harvesting Code Conjurer		♦	It uses the ranking given by Merobase.
	CodeGenie	♦	♦	It uses the ranking given by Sourcerer.
Reuse Opportun ity Recomme nder	CodeBroker		♦	The ranking is calculated based on the relevance of a component to the task-at-hand. This relevance is determined by the conceptual similarity between the comments and identifiers in the program being developed and the textual documents of components in the repository. The relevance is also determined by the signature compatibility between the signatures of programs under development and those of components. It uses Latent Semantic Analysis for indexing and retrieval.
	Rascal		♦	The tool predicts a user's vote that represents the likelihood of a reuse opportunity for any method in the component library based on the developer's current preferences. The ranking is based on the method's predicted vote. The higher the vote, the higher the ranking.
General Purpose Search Engine	Google	♦		It uses more than 200 signals, including the PageRank™ algorithm, to examine the entire link structure of the Web and determine which pages are most important. It also conducts hypertext-matching analysis to determine which pages are relevant to the specific search being conducted. By combining overall importance and query-specific relevance, Google is able to put the most relevant and reliable results first.
Others	JIRISS		♦	It calculates a similarity measure between each document in the semantic search space and the user query. The semantic search space contains comments, identifiers, and structural information extracted from the source code at the class or method level. The ranking is based on this similarity measure and the higher the similarity, the higher the ranking.
	Codetrail			

6.2.2 Additional Information for each Match

Tools also show additional information about each result that could help users make informed decisions about the relevance and suitability of matches. The information showed can be grouped in six groups: functionality, license, support, level of activity, quality, and reputation. The first four groups have been reported as selection criteria of open source components most commonly used by developers [59]. Quality and reputation are also some criteria to select source code components that have been reported by Chen et al [8]. We classified the information showed by tools in these six groups of characteristics by answering the following questions written from the developer's point of view. Table 15 summarizes our analysis.

Functionality	Does the source code satisfy my functional requirements?
License	Are the terms and conditions for use, reproduction, modification, distribution, and redistribution of the source code appropriate for my project?
Support	Does the community associated with this source code will help me answer questions about how to use the source code? Will they help me solve problems with the source code?
Level of Activity	Is there an active developer or community behind the source code?
Quality	Is the source code reliable, usable, efficient, maintainable, and portable?
Reputation	Does this source code have a good reputation among the community?

6.2.2.1 Functionality

Most of the tools, except Agora, Gilligan, Jigsaw, Google, and Codetrail, help developers evaluate results by showing the functionality of a match. In most of the cases, the tools present the functionality using code snippets, or the source code file. There are some tools that show functionality in other ways. Strathcona, Maracatu, and Maracatu + folksonomy present a UML diagram of the component accompanied by the code snippet. Mica shows the functionality using Web Pages that contain source code or official documentation. The tool shows a Java icon to identify pages that has source code and a Javadoc icon to identify pages that has official documentation. Assieme accompanies matches with jar files, a list of Java types and libraries used in the match. SourceForge, Tigris, and Github, project-hosting sites, show the functionality by including a short text description of the project.

6.2.2.2 License

Seven tools show information about the license of the source code. Koders and Sourcerer show a short text with the name of the license of the code snippet. Google Code Search, Krugle, SourceForge, and Tigris show also a short text with the name of the license, but this text is a link to a Web page that explains the terms of the license. S6 includes a button to access information about the license of each code snippet.

6.2.2.3 Support

There are two types of support: usage support, and failure support or maintenance [60]. Having usage support will allow users to get some answers to questions about the use of the software. The failure support or maintenance is related to the fact that users can get help to solve problems in the software.

Four of the analyzed tools, Krugle, SourceForge, Tigris, Github, show information related to these two types of support. These tools show if the projects have mailing lists, forums, and technical support to be used in case usage support is needed. In case failure support is required, these tools show if the projects have bug trackers, technical support, and patches.

6.2.2.4 Level of Activity

The level of activity of software consists of community activity and developer activity [60]. Six tools, SPARS-J, Krugle, Merobase, SourceForge, Tigris, Github, show information about the level of activity. These tools provide community activity information by giving Web traffic, number of download, number of bugs opened/closed, feature request, patches, support requests, and forum traffic. In addition, these tools provide developer activity information by giving CVS/SVN activity, number of developers, bug trackers statistics, patches, and support requests.

6.2.2.5 Quality

According to the ISO9126-1 software quality model [30], there are six main quality characteristics:

- Functionality: suitability, accurateness, interoperability, compliance, security
- Reliability: maturity, fault tolerance, recoverability
- Usability: understandability, learnability, operability
- Efficiency: time behavior, resource behavior
- Maintainability: analyzability, changeability, stability, testability
- Portability: adaptability, installability, conformance, replaceability

When analyzing if the tools showed information about quality, we consider only the last five characteristics because the first one, functionality, has been considered separately in our analysis.

Only one tool, SourceForge, showed some information related with software quality. This tool shows the GUI screenshot of the project which falls into the usability category.

6.2.2.6 Reputation

Reputation is defined as "what is generally said or believed about a person's or thing's character or standing" [43]. We consider that a source code has good reputation when it has a good number of users, and other members of the community have recommended it.

SourceForge shows reputation information using ratings and reviews. Users of this tool can give "thumbs up" or "thumbs down" by clicking on a graphical representation of these concepts. Users can also write a review about their experience with the software. The tool will show the percentage of users that recommended this project based on the users that rated it. It will also show graphically the number of thumbs up in blue and the number of thumbs down in red, as shown in Figure 6.

Figure 6. SourceForge Rate and Review Feature

Github allows users to "follow" other users and "watch" projects. For each match of users and projects, it shows how many followers and watchers they have respectively, as seen in Figure 7.

Figure 7. Github Watchers and Followers Feature

6.2.2.7 Others

Twelve tools show additional information with the match that does not fall in any of the previous categories. Strathcona and CodeBroker provide additional rationale that explains why that match is showed in a certain position. Koders, Google Code Search, Krugle, and Github show information about the languages that are present in project. This is shown as a list of languages or as a bar graph showing the representation of each language in the source code. SPARS-J, Sourcerer, and Merobase show additional information about package metrics, fingerprints, and source code metrics such as line of code or ratio of comments per lines of source code. STeP_IN_Java offers users the possibility to read discussion archives and also ask question to experts during the evaluation of matches. In addition, Koders shows the development cost for a project simulating it is being built from scratch. Github shows a project summary and statistics powered by Ohloh. Finally, Extreme Harvesting and Code Conjurer only show results that pass the specified test cases.

Table 17. Additional Information Showed for Each Match by Tools

Tool Goal	Tool Name	Functionality	License	Support	Level of Activity	Quality	Reputation	Others
API Example Oriented Code Search	Prospector	♦						
	Strathcona	♦						Rationale of relevance
	JSearch	♦						
	MAPO	♦						
	Mica	♦						
	XSnippet	♦						
	PARSEWeb	♦						
	STeP_IN_Java	♦						Discussion archive Ask question to expert
	Assieme	♦						
	XFinder	♦						
	SNIFF	♦						
Web-based Code Search Engine	Agora							
	Koders	♦	♦					Development costs for project Languages in project
	SPARS-J	♦			♦			Package metrics
	Google Code Search	♦	♦					Language
	Krugle	♦	♦	♦	♦			Languages in project
	Sourcerer	♦	♦					Source code fingerprints
	Merobase	♦			♦			Source

Tool Goal	Tool Name	Functionality	License	Support	Level of Activity	Quality	Reputation	Others
								code metrics
Component Retrieval	Maracatu	♦						
	Maracatu + Folksonomy	♦						
	B.A.R.T.	♦						
Integration/Transformation	Gilligan							
	Jigsaw							
	S⁶	♦	♦					
Project-hosting Sites	SourceForge	♦	♦	♦	♦	♦	♦	
	Tigris	♦	♦	♦	♦			
	Github	♦		♦	♦		♦	Languages in project Project summary and statistics provided by Ohloh
Test-Driven Code Search	Extreme Harvesting	♦						It only shows the results that have the exact signature, compile, and pass test cases
	Code Conjurer	♦						It only shows the components that pass test cases
	CodeGenie	♦						
Reuse Opportunity	CodeBroker	♦						Words that contribut

Tool Goal	Tool Name	Functionality	License	Support	Level of Activity	Quality	Reputation	Others
Recommender								ed to relevance between the component and the task at hand
	Rascal	◆						
General Purpose Search Engine	Google							
Others	JIRISS	◆						
	Codetrail							

6.3 Summary

Empirical studies report that developers use different criteria to evaluate source code candidates depending on the search target. When developers look for code snippets on the Web they mainly evaluate results based on the functionality and cosmetic features, such as the presence of source code and the low incidence of advertisement. When developers look for open source components and projects on the Web, they use multiple criteria to evaluate candidates. The most important evaluation criterion is the compliance with functionality requirements, followed by licensing, usability/component characteristics, costs, user support available, and level of project activity. Familiarity with an already used component was the most important criteria when resources and time are limited. Other criteria also reported by empirical studies include: architectural compliance, reputation of components and supplier, quality of documentation, and environment or platform.

Developers make mainly two types of judgments while choosing a result: relevance judgments and suitability judgments. The former is used to identify promising candidates and the latter is used to define if a promising candidate is appropriate to solve the user's development problem. More empirical studies are needed to observe the evaluation criteria and strategies used by developers for the different types of source code needs. Additional empirical studies can also be helpful to study the characteristics of relevance and suitability judgments. Studies could also verify the presence of the correlation between the emphasis of relevance and suitability judgments, and the certainty level of expected results implied from analyzing previous empirical studies.

Tools mainly support two approaches to help developers evaluate the results: ranking and showing additional information about results. Most of the tools use ranking, and about half of them uses source code structure characteristics to rank results. Most of the tools show source code to help developers understand the functionality but only few tools show other type of additional information that could help developer make informed decisions. The additional information that tools show includes license, support, level of activity, quality, reputation, and others. We observed that few tools show additional information regarding quality and reputation. There is a lack of tools that show different characteristics of the results in a way that could make the user take rapid and informed decisions, maybe using graphic representations.

Chapter 7: Use Suitable Results

After developers select a relevant and suitable source code result, they need to integrate the source code into their current knowledge or development environment. In this section, we analyze empirical studies that examine how developers use the results for different types of source code needs. We also evaluate the level of support that tools provide to help developers use source code found on the Web.

7.1 Empirical Results

Once developers find a suitable piece of source code on the Web, they need to integrate it to their current knowledge or their current source code to solve the software development problem that motivated the search. We are aware of three empirical studies that report on how developers use source code after the evaluation process. One of them [4] reports on how developers use code snippets after they are found and two of them [8, 37] report on how developers use open source components and projects after they are selected. We first analyze how developers use code snippets found on the Web and then how they use open source software.

7.1.1 Code Snippets

Brandt et al. provides some evidence on how developers use code snippets on the Web to learn, clarify, remember, and fix bugs as summarized in Table 18.

Table 18. Use of Suitable Results by Type of Source Code Need

Need		Source Code Use
Reminder	For syntactic programming language details	View search result or API documentation to remember syntax
	For routinely-used functionality	Copy and paste lines of code
Examples to Clarify	How to implement functionality in a specific programming language	Copy, paste, and adapt code to their needs Developers trust code and they will not immediately test the copied code Developers make minor mistakes while adapting code
Conceptual Learning		Learning by doing: developers often immediately begin experimenting with code samples in tutorials Developers often copy, paste, and adapt code before understanding how it worked and reading the tutorial Developers copy approximately 10 lines at a time
Bug Fix		Developers use the information found to fix the bug even without understanding the reason

Often the snippets of source code found on the Web are copied and pasted to the developer's environment. When developers are learning a new concept, they start experimenting with the source code in tutorials even before they read the tutorial or understand the source code. This experimentation will help developers understand the concept without reading the tutorial or to identify challenging sections of the code that could be understood by reading specific parts of the tutorial. Developers also copy and paste source code from the Web when they are trying to clarify how to implement functionality in a specific programming language. Developers will adapt the copied source code to their needs but they will make some small mistakes such as not replacing all the occurrences of the name of a variable. These errors will not be easy to find because developers trust the copied source code and they do not test it immediately. Developers also copy and paste code from the Web to remember routinely-used functionality. Certain functionality is used many times by developers such as connecting to a database. However, developers do not consider that is worthy to memorize it and they just copy and paste it every time from the Web. Developers also copy and paste snippets of source code that help them fix a bug. Often a solution to a bug can be found on the Web, and developers use the information, that could be source code or any advice, to fix the bug. Sometimes copy and paste is not necessary and it is enough for developer to see the search results or a piece of source code to, for example, remember syntactic programming language details.

It is interesting to see how the Web is changing the way we learn and the level of understanding we need to solve a problem. Developers often need to learn a new concept to complete a development task, they usually look for tutorials to learn, but when they find source code in tutorials, they start to experiment with it. Developers will adapt the source code and test it, if it works correctly and solves the development problem, developers will sometimes not bother reading the tutorial any further. It is up to the developers to understand the concept based on the adapted source code or to defer the understanding and learning aspect. Similarly, when developers fix a bug based on the solutions provided on the Web, often developers just apply the solution without really understanding what the cause of the problem was. The benefit of this phenomenon is that developers are more efficient in that they solve problems quicker, but the disadvantage is that if they do not understand the concepts it would be difficult for them to apply it in another context or related problem. It is also interesting to see the high reliance that developers have on the Web. They use the Web as a memory aid to remember syntactic details or frequently used code snippets. Developers decide not to remember these details because the Web will always be there to help them remember.

7.1.2   Open Source Components & Projects

Chen et al. and Madanmohan and De' studied how open source components and projects are used after they are selected. Both studies agree in that it is very common to adapt the open source software to integrate it to the software developer environment. Chen et al. reported that 45% of questionnaire participants needed to change the source code to fix bugs. This seems to be a very high percentage and could mean that the quality of open source software is not good. However, we expect the quality of open source to improve over the years as reported by the Coverity Report [11]. It was also reported that 39% of participants make changes for other reasons. These other reasons could include customization and integration changes.

In addition to source code adaptation, Madanmohand and De' also reported that sometimes developers contact the author of source code to seek permission for use and extension. In other cases, developers do not look at the source code even though they have access to it. This happens when developers do not need to modify the source code and the software teams do not have enough resources (knowledge, skills, manpower) to do it.

7.2   Tools

We analyzed the tools presented in section 2.3 to determine the support they provide the users to use and integrate the suitable results they found to their task at hand. Few tools, only seven out of thirty five, provide some help to incorporate the found source code in the user's project. These tools mostly help developers adapt source code and/or integrate it to the user's source code as shown in Table 19.

Table 19. Use of Suitable Results Supported by Tools

Support for Using Suitable Results	Tools
Source Code Adaptation	Prospector, Strathcona, S6
Source Code Integration	Gilligan, Jigsaw, Code Conjurer, CodeGenie

7.2.1   Source Code Adaptation

Adaptation is the activity of changing the found source code, so it will fit better with the user's project. Three tools, Prospector, Strathcona, and S6, provide support for source code adaptation. Prospector adapts the returned source code so that it references to variables in the user's program. Strathcona returns snippets of source code that are structurally similar to the user's code. S6 applies different types of transformations to the source code in order to show code snippets that match the user's specification. Transformations include changes in the source code to match signatures, to assure that the code compiles, to assure that the code passes the specified test case among others.

7.2.2 Source Code Integration

Four tools, Gilligan, Jigsaw, Code Conjurer, and CodeGenie, help developers integrate the source code they found into the source code that they are currently working on. Gilligan and Jigsaw are both tools that specialize on the integration of source code and not in source code search. Gilligan identifies which dependencies in the source code being reused are already satisfied in the project where it is being integrated. The tool allows developers to record their decisions about how they want to deal with the dependencies using a visual reuse plan. Similarly, Jigsaw supports the integration of source code but at a smaller scale. Developers identify the method they want to copy and the method where they want to integrate the source code. The tool analyzes the structure of both pieces of source code, performs the integration, and shows the integrated source code with different colors to indicate the decisions taken by the tool and to signal possible areas of concern.

Code Conjurer and CodeGenie are test-driven code search tools that return code that passes the specified test cases and help the user integrate it into the source code he/she is currently working on. Code Conjurer weaves the chosen result directly into the developer project by automatically resolving its dependencies. CodeGenie copies all classes inside the chosen code result into the developer's project and merges classes with coincident names.

7.3 Summary

Empirical studies show that developers use source code found on the Web in different ways depending on the search target. When developers use code snippets from the Web, sometimes it is enough for them to just look at the results to, for example, remember syntactic programming language details. Developers also copy and paste some lines of code, which could be adapted, or not depending on their needs. When developers use open source components and projects, they often modify the source code to fix bugs or for other reasons, and sometimes they also contact the author of the source code to ask for permission to use it. In some cases, developers do not look at the source code because they do not need to modify it and the software team does not have enough resources to do it. More empirical studies are needed to understand how developers use source code found on the Web to satisfy their different source code needs.

Few tools, only seven out of 35, offer adequate support to use source code found on the Web. These tools offer support mainly by helping developers adapt and integrate source code. Three tools offer support to adapt the source code before presenting it to the user. These tools change the found source code so that it will fit better the user environment, for example, changing names of variables to match users' program or making transformation to match user specifications. Four tools offer support to integrate source code into the developers' environment by identifying dependencies between two projects or two snippets of source code, by helping record integration decisions, or by automatically resolving dependencies.

Chapter 8: Discussion and Future Work

In this section, we discuss how the analysis of tools and empirical studies helped us better understand the problem of source code seeking on the Web. We learned that the size of the search target matters. Based on that observation, we analyzed how well the empirical studies and tools have covered each target size without our Model of Source Code Seeking on the Web. Lastly, the future work is also discussed in this section.

8.1   Size of the search target matters

We identified two types of search targets according to their size. Code snippets are in the first category. Code snippets are blocks of source code and could include from one to dozens of lines of code, but they are always smaller than an entire class or source file. We include in the second category both components and open source projects, because the ways in which people interact with and search for these are similar. Components can vary in size from a single class to a set of files that work together, such as jar files. In contrast, open source projects can consist of one or more software components. Table 20 shows the types of tools that support each target size, as well as how developers evaluate and use results organized by target size.

Table 20. Types of Tools, Evaluation Criteria, and Use of Results by Search Target Size

Search Target Size	Type of Tools	Empirical Studies on Evaluation Criteria	Empirical Studies on Use of Results
Code Snippets	- API example oriented code search - Web-based code search - Integration/transformation - Reuse opportunity recommender - Project-hosting sites - Test-driven code search - General purpose search engine	- Functionality - Quality based on cosmetic features	- Look at the results - Copy and paste as-is - Copy and paste and adapt
Open Source Components and Projects	- Web-based code search - Component Retrieval - Integration/transformation - Project-hosting sites - Test-driven code search - API example oriented code search - General purpose search engine	- Functionality - License - Support - Level of activity - Quality - Reputation - Integration costs - Architectural compatibility	- Reference examples - Reuse as-is - Reuse and adapt

8.1.1 Code Snippets

Developers look for code snippets or lines of code to learn how to use an API, to acquire a new concept, or to remind them of syntax. Developers expect to find some lines of code that they could copy and paste with or without the need to adapt the code to integrate it to their current development task. The types of tools that mainly support developers looking for code snippets are API example oriented code search, web-based code search, integration/transformation, and reuse opportunity recommenders. Many of these tools, especially the first and last ones in the list, make use of the current context of the user to suggest potentially related code snippets. Few tools in the project-hosting sites, test-driven code search, and general-purpose search engine group also help developers look for code snippets. Many tools in the listed groups support both code snippets and open source components & projects, but only the reuse opportunity recommender group supports exclusively code snippets. When developers evaluate the result set given by the tools, they mainly pay attention to the functionality of the code snippet. In this case, developers do not need to worry much about licenses, support, reputation, and other criteria. Developers mainly use the code snippets by copying and pasting, and making some adaptations to the lines of code. Not many tools offer support to integrate code snippets, mainly, because they assume developers will copy and paste them.

8.1.2   Open Source Components & Projects

Developers look for open source components and projects when they want to reuse complete libraries, algorithms, frameworks, or systems. These open source components and projects are also used as examples or reference for a future implementation. Developers expect to find complete components or systems that they could reuse, but the expectation changes according to what they find available on the Web. The types of tools that mainly support developers seeking open source components and projects are Web-based code search, component retrieval, integration/transformation, test-driven code search, and project-hosting sites. Only few of these tools take into consideration the current development context of the developer to suggest components or to help in the evaluation of results. Also, only few tools in the API example oriented code search and general-purpose search engine group help developers look for open source components & projects. Many tools in the listed groups support both code snippets and open source components & projects, but only the component retrieval group supports exclusively open source components & projects. When developers evaluate open source components and projects, they look not only at the functionality, but also at other aspects such as compatibility of the license, the support and level of activity of the open source community in case of problems and questions, the quality of the software, and the reputation of the developers. After selecting a suitable component or project, developers will adapt their current code, and possibly the found code, to integrate them. There are few tools that help developers facilitate this integration.

The problem of source code seeking on the Web has very different assumptions and characteristics depending on the size of search target. We find that looking for code snippets on the Web and looking for open source components and systems represent two sets of different problems that are worth investigating separately.

8.2   Empirical Studies

Based on our observation that the search target matters (recall Section 8.1), we organized the empirical results presented in sections 3.1, 4.1, 5.1, 6.1, and 7.1 in three groups: the ones that focus on: i) how people look for code snippets only, ii) how developers look for open source components & projects, and iii) how developers look for both code snippets and open source components & projects. For each group, we analyzed the extent to which each stage of our Model of Source Code Seeking on the Web is covered by the empirical studies. Figure 8 shows a bar chart for each phase of our model. Each bar chart has three bars and a vertical scale from 1-10. The bars show the number of empirical studies done to study how developers look for snippets only (first bar), open source components & projects only (second bar), and both snippets and open source components & projects (third bar). We found that there are few empirical studies that focus on the phenomenon of looking for source code on the Web. Also, more empirical studies are needed for all the stages of our model, especially ones to identify how developers evaluate and use the source code they find on the Web.

Even though the number of empirical studies found for the stages related to identify source code need, translate and form need to Web resource, and evaluate results is the same; the emphasis and amount of information they give related to each stage is different. There are some empirical studies focused on identifying the needs of developers such as the study done by Umarji et al. [59] and other studies that focused on the translation of needs to Web resource such as the log analysis done by Bajracharya and Lopes [1]. However, the empirical studies related to the evaluation of results were not mainly focused on this aspect, and as a consequence they report minimal data on how developers evaluate source code results. For that reason, we argue that more empirical studies are needed to better understand how developers evaluate source code results.

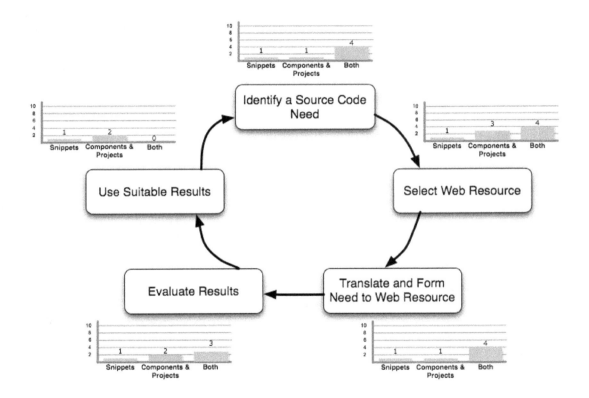

Figure 8. Empirical Studies Done for each Stage of the Model of Source Code Seeking on the Web

Few empirical studies focus on how developers look for source code on the Web. We reviewed the literature and found eight of them. Only one empirical study focuses on how developers look specifically for code snippets on the Web, but it covers all the five stages of our source code seeking model. Three empirical studies focus on how developers look for open source components and projects on the Web. However, none of them covers all the five stages of our model. Finally, four empirical studies focus on how developers look for both code snippets and open source components and projects and none of them reported on how the source code found was used by developers.

Identify a Source Code Need. Six empirical studies reported on developers' source code needs. These studies include two that reported on search engines logs [1, 21], two on laboratory experiments [51, 55], one on questionnaires [8, 59], and one on a search engine log and a laboratory experiment [4]. Most of these studies reported only on the motivation of developers and some only on the search targets. More empirical studies are needed to identify source code needs based on both the motivation and search targets. Having only the motivation or search targets does not provide a specific understanding of the need due to the fact that different search targets can be used with the same motivation. None of these studies was performed on field sites to identify the source code needs that arise while developers perform their daily work activities.

Select Web Resource. All the empirical studies in our survey reported on the Web Resources that developers used to find source code on the Web. These studies reported that developers typically use general-purpose search engines such as Google. Other Web resources used include project-hosting sites, source code search engines, official sites for documentation, mailing lists, forums, and corporate portals. However, few empirical studies reported on which Web Resources are more suitable for different source code need motivations and targets. These studies also reported that the selection of a Web Resource is influenced by the developer's domain knowledge, past experience, and social interactions.

Translate and Form Need to Web Resource. Six studies reported on how developers translate their needs to Web Resources. All these studies observed that developers use query formulation, two observed the use of query reformulation, and only one observed the use of browsing. Empirical studies showed a good set of query samples that are used when developers are looking for source code. However, there is the need to relate those queries with developers' needs. Empirical studies are needed to understand how developers interact with Web Resources beyond the keyword box to look for source code. It would be useful if these studies could be done also in work environments.

Evaluate Results. Six empirical studies reported on how developers evaluate results when they are searching for source code. These studies revealed that when developers are looking for code snippets, they make decisions based on the functionality of the source code and also based on cosmetic features, such as few commercial advertisements on the web site as an indicator of high quality. When developers are looking for open source components or projects, they evaluate source code based on functionality, license, usability, cost issues related with integration, user support, level of activity, familiarity, architectural compliance, reputation, quality of documentation, and environment or platform. There have been no laboratory studies or field observations of the process that developers follow to evaluate results, especially for open source components and projects. Factors in the evaluation process include the time they spend on it, the biases developer's have, and how the evaluation is related to a particular information need.

Use Suitable Results. Three studies reported on how developers use the results they selected from the search. These studies show that when developers are seeking code snippets, sometimes they only look at the results; sometimes they copy and paste the code; or they copy and paste and experiment with it by adapting it. When developers look for open source components and projects, they sometimes use them as reference examples and other times they reuse the source code. When developers reuse the components or projects, they have to fix bugs and change the component's source code to fit their specific needs.

Studies have also reported that developers sometimes contact the authors of the source code asking for permission to make changes. In some cases, developers do not need to look at the source code because there is no need for changes, or there are not enough resources to do it. More empirical studies are needed to better understand how developers use the source code they find on the Web for the different source code needs they have. This information can be useful for tool builders since most of the tools do not include support for the use of source code found on the Web.

8.3   Tool Support

Based on our evaluation of tools presented in sections 3.2, 4.2, 5.2, 6.2, and 7.2, we analyzed and estimated how well these tools support each of the stages of our Model of Source Code Seeking on the Web. We found that few tools help developers identify a source code need and use suitable results. Also, we observed that most of the tools offer help to evaluate results but the level of support is low.

We organized the tools by the size of the search target they support according to our discussion in 8.1. Table 21 shows this classification. In the first group, we have 12 out of 35 tools that help developers seek code snippets only. In the second group, we have again 12 tools that help seek open source components & projects. In the third group, we have 11 tools that help developer seek both: code snippets, and open source components & projects. Figure 9, that shows the results of our analysis, includes a bar chart with three bars for each stage of our model. Each of the bars belongs to one of the three groups of tools we just described. Next, we present the observations of our tool support analysis.

Table 21. Tool Classification by Search Target Size

	Snippets	Open Source Components and Projects	Both
API Example Oriented Code Search	Prospector, Strathcona, MAPO, Mica, PARSEWeb, STeP_IN_Java, XSnippet, SNIFF	JSearch, XFinder	Assieme
Web-based Code Search Engine		Agora, SPARS_J	Koders, Google Code Search, Krugle, Sourcerer, Merobase
Component Retrieval		Maracatu, Maracatu + Folksonomy, B.A.R.T.	
Integration/Transformation	Jigsaw	Gilligan	S6
Project-hosting Sites		SourceForge, Tigris	Github
Test-Driven Code Search		Code Conjurer, CodeGenie	Extreme Harvesting
Reuse Opportunity Recommender	CodeBroker, Rascal		
General Purpose Search Engine			Google
Others	Codetrail		JIRISS

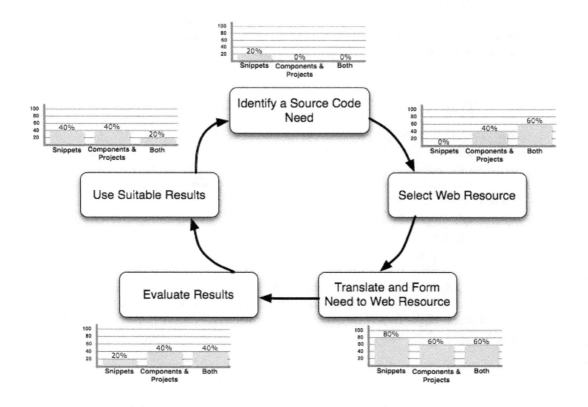

Figure 9. Tool Support for each Stage of the Model of Source Code Seeking on the Web

Identify a Source Code Need. Few tools help developers identify a source code need. Most of these tools are the ones that help developers search for only code snippets. Typically, tools in this group are integrated into IDEs and they use the current development context to identify a potential need. Tools in the Components & Projects and Both groups, assume that developers identify their source code needs by themselves, so do not offer automated support. These two groups of tools, which include more web-based tools than the Snippet group, could benefit from using the current developer context to suggest potential source code needs. However, the integration between the web environment and the developer's environment remains a challenge.

Select Web Resource. Tools that help developers search for both snippets and open source components & projects offer better support to the developer to select a Web resource to be used as a starting point of the search. Tools in this group include most of the ones that act as Web Brokers and Web Sites. Tools that act as Web Brokers offer better support to developers to select a web resource compared to tools that act a Web Sites. This is the case because tools that act as Web Brokers offer more diverse options, including tutorials, forums, blogs, among others. In contrast, tools that act as Web Sites only show results that are limited to web pages in the same Web Site. Having a wider variety of resources to choose from can help developers be aware and take advantage of different sources of information that could satisfy their source code needs. For example, when looking for a bug fix, a solution can be posted in forums, blogs, or other different sources. Tools in the Snippet group do not help developers choose a Web Resource because most of them offer source code options based on their local repository and not directly from the Web. Tools that help developers look for only open source components and projects offer less support to select a Web Resource than tools in the Both group but more than tools in the Snippets group. This is so because almost the same number of tools in the Components & Project group acts as Web Sites and local repositories.

Translate and Form Need to Web Resource. Most of the tools offer good support to translate and form a need to Web Resources. Almost all the tools offer support for query formulation and few for query reformulation, browsing, and automatic translation. Tools that help developers look only for code snippets offer more support to translate the need than tools in the Components & Projects and Both groups. This is so because half of the tools in the Snippets group offer automatic translation of needs, which is done using the current context of the developer in an IDE.

Evaluate Results. Tools offer little support for evaluating the results. In all the three groups, there was only minimal support for the evaluation of results. Tools in the Snippets group offer less support than the other two groups, because tools in this group show mainly only the ranking and source code of the results as information to evaluate the options. However, tools in the other two groups also show additional information such as licenses, reputation, and technical support among others, along with the ranking. We expected that tools in the Snippets group would have less support for evaluation because developers looking for source code snippets mainly evaluate them based on the functionality and no other criteria. We observe that the support of tools in the Components & Projects and Both groups could be improved to show additional information that developers often use to evaluate source code such as quality, level of support, integration cost among others, and also show this additional information in a way that could be easy to use and understand during the evaluation.

Use Suitable Results. Few tools help developers use the suitable results. Only 7 out of 35 support this activity, but all of them do a thorough job. In general, it seems that tools designers have overlooked the integration of the source code results into the developer's environment. We expect to see more tools in the future that help with integration; especially the tools for Components & Projects, where integration often requires more effort than for code snippets. Similar to the Identification of the Source Code Need stage, the integration of results from the Web to the developer environment (commonly an IDE) remains a challenge.

8.4 Future work

After reviewing the literature, we found that the phenomenon of source code seeking on the Web has received little attention from the research community so far. The existence of few empirical studies in this area shows that this area can be further explored. Also, the analyzed tools do not sufficiently support all the stages of the Model of Source Code Seeking on the Web. This fact suggests that extensive research needs to be done to improve the tools.

Empirical studies are needed to better understand each of the stages of the proposed Model of Source Code Seeking on the Web. The empirical studies should rely on direct observation of professionals in industrial environments. Laboratory experiments, questionnaires, focus groups, or other techniques can be informative as well. All of these techniques could be applied to answer the following questions:

Identify a Source Code Need	What motivates developers to look for source code on the Web? What is the size of the source code target developers expect to find? How the motivation and the source code target relate to each other to form a source code need?
Select Web Resource	Which Web resources are more suitable starting points when searching for different source code needs? What aspects, such as domain knowledge, past experience, and social interactions, influence the decision of which Web resources developers use to start a source code search?
Translate and Form Need to Web Resource	How developers interact with Web resources beyond using the keyword box to look for source code?
Evaluate Results	What is the process followed by developers to evaluate results? What information is used to make relevance and suitability judgments? How does the evaluation process differ among source code needs? What biases do developers have during the evaluation of results? What source code characteristics could be used to improve the ranking of results? What additional information and how it can be shown along with the results to help developers make better decisions faster? When developers don't find what they need, how do they decided to stop?
Use Suitable Results	How developers use the source code they found on the Web for different source code needs? How does the reused source code affect the evolution of the project?

Our literature survey also revealed that tools that support source code seeking on the Web are in need of improvement, especially tools that help developers look for open source components and projects. This kind of tools could be improved by offering support for automatic identification of needs and automatic translation of needs. This automation could be done by using the current context of the user, as is done for tools that help developers look for code snippets. These tools can also be improved by presenting additional information that is useful during the evaluation process such as source code quality, level of support, and integration cost. This additional information should be presented in a way that would be easier to understand and compare during the evaluation process. Tools that help developers look for code snippets, open source components, and projects can be improved by increasing the level of support provided to integrate the source code found on the Web and the current developer's environment.

One of the approaches that could be used to implement the integration between the current context of the user and web-based tools to look for open source components and projects is to create a Firefox add-on that allows the Web browser to communicate with the IDE environment. Such integration was implemented in Codetrail to improve developer's use of Web resources by connecting Eclipse IDE and Firefox web browser. This add-on could allow developers to select the components and projects they would like to evaluate from a web-based tool such as SourceForge. The add-on can access to the current context of the user in an IDE environment, such as the Eclipse workspace. Having access to the source code of projects and the current project in Eclipse allows the add-on to analyze license conflicts, libraries or frameworks in common, similarities in coding styles, and possible steps for integration. The information returned by the tool can help developers make better decisions about the suitability of a component or system during the evaluation process and it can also help with the integration process. In addition, the integration with the current context of the user can be used to automatically identify potential information needs. The tool could be implemented as an Eclipse plug-in, but a Firefox plug-in would be more effective because the developer would not need to switch between contexts for searching and for coding.

Chapter 9: Conclusion

The increased availability and quality of open source code on the Web is changing the way software developers write source code. Developers are using the Web as a huge source code repository to look for source code they could reuse to solve a software development problem. We call this phenomenon, source code seeking on the Web. It is important to understand how developers look for source code on the Web so that tools and approaches can be suggested to better support their needs.

This survey proposes a five-stage model that describes the stages developers follow to find source code on the Web. These stages include: identify source code need, select Web resource, translate need to Web resource, evaluate results, and use suitable results. We made an extensive review of the literature to evaluate the empirical studies done for each stage and to evaluate how well the tools support each stage. We present the results of our analysis by answering the questions that were posed in the introduction:

Identify Source Code Need

- What are the source code needs that make developers look for source code on the Web?

Developers look for source code on the Web mainly for seven purposes: (1) to reuse source code as-is for wrappers, parsers, small functionality, data structures, algorithms, GUI widgets, API/libraries, and systems; (2) to find examples of usage for GUI widgets or API/libraries; (3) to remember syntactic programming language details or frequently used functionality; (4) to find examples to clarify how to implement functionality in a specific language, or how to implement an algorithm or data structure; (5) to learn unfamiliar concepts; (6) to fix a bug; and (7) to get ideas to implement a new system.

- How well do the tools help developers identify their source code needs?

Only few tools offer a good level of support to identify source code needs. Four out of 35 tools help developers automatically identify their source code needs. Most of these tools help developers look for code snippets; they are integrated with an IDE; and they use the developer's context to suggest source code needs.

Select Web Resource

- Which Web resources software developers use to start looking for source code on the Web?

Developers mainly use general-purpose search engines such as Google to start looking for source code on the Web. They also use, in a lesser extend, project-hosting sites, source code search engines, official documentation sites, mailing lists, forums, and blogs.

- How well do the tools help developers select a Web resource to start looking for source code on the Web?

Tools offer an acceptable level of support to select a Web resource that can be used as a starting point to look for source code on the Web. Tools that act as Web Brokers offer good support because they show diverse Web Sites that could satisfy developers' source code needs. Tools that act as Web Sites offer moderate support because they show only Web Pages that belong the same Web Site, there is not much variety to choose from. Tools that act as Wrappers of Web Resource also offer moderate support because these tools choose the Web resource that they will use. Finally, tools that act as Repositories offer no support to select a Web resource because all of them show results from local repositories. We did not find any tool that would perform a search using several search tools in parallel to show comparative results, as is done for example for airline tickets.

Translate and Form Need to Web Resource

- How do developers translate their source code needs to Web resources?

Developers mainly translate their source code needs by formulating queries in domain vocabulary, implementation vocabulary, or a combination of both. Developers use natural language when they are trying to learn new concepts or fix a bug. Programming language is used when developers want to remember syntactic details or frequently used functionality. A combination of natural and programming language is used for all the other reported source code needs. Developers reformulate their queries based on the initial results they obtained. Browsing is another technique used to translate developers' source code need, but it is not commonly used due to the fact that not many tools implement this feature.

- How well do the tools help developers translate their source code needs?

Tools offer a good level of support that helps developers translate their source code needs. Almost all the tools support query reformation, and some of them also help select keywords and connectors to form the query. Few tools support query reformation, browsing, and automatic translation of needs based on the context of the user.

Evaluate Results

- How do developers evaluate the source code candidates to determine which is the most relevant and suitable for their source code needs?

Developers evaluate source code candidates differently depending on the size of the search target. When developers look for code snippets, they evaluate the functionality and quality based on cosmetic features. When developers look for open source components and projects, they evaluate functionality, license, support, level of activity, quality, reputation, cost issues related with integration, and architectural compatibility.

- How well do the tools support developers in evaluating and selecting the most relevant and suitable result for their source code needs?

Tools offer a very limited support to evaluate source code results. Tools help with the evaluation by ranking the results and by showing additional information about results. Almost all the tools support ranking and around half of them uses the code structure properties to rank results. The additional information that tools show about results includes license, support, level of activity, quality, reputation, and others. Only few tools show additional information regarding quality and reputation.

Use Suitable Results

- How do developers use source code found on the Web?

Developers use results differently depending on the search target. When developers look for code snippets, they copy and paste the code as-is, or copy and past and adapt it, or sometimes it is enough for them to just look at the selected result. When developers look for open source components and projects, they use the selected results as reference example or they reuse the code as-is, or they reuse the code and adapt it.

- How well do the tools support developers to use source code found on the Web?

Only few tools offer a good level of support to use source code found on the Web. Only 7 out of 35 tools help developers adapt and/or integrate the selected source code into their software development tasks. This lack of support is evident in tools that help developers look for code snippets and also for tools that help look for open source components and projects.

This survey shows that the phenomenon of source code seeking on the Web is beginning to receive attention in the research community. There are lots of opportunities to increase our understanding of this phenomenon by conducting empirical studies, in particular, to study how developers evaluate source code results and how they use the source code found in industrial settings. Similarly, a lot more can be done to improve tools, in particular, to expand the support they offer developers to identify source code needs, evaluate source code results, and use source code found on the Web.

References

[1]   Bajracharya S. and Lopes C., "Mining Search Topics from a Code Search Engine Usage Log," in *Proceedings of the 6th IEEE Working Conference on Mining Software Repositories*, Los Alamitos, CA, USA, 2009, pp. 111-120.

[2]   Bates M. J., "The Design of Browsing and Berrypicking Techniques for the Online Search Interface," *Online Review,* vol. 13, pp. 407-424, 1989.

[3]   Beck K., *Test-Driven Development: By Example*: Addison-Wesley Professional, 2003.

[4]   Brandt J., Guo P. J., Lewenstein J., Dontcheva M., and Klemmer S. R., "Two Studies of Opportunistic Programming: Interleaving Web Foraging, Learning, and Writing Code," in *Proceedings of the 27th international conference on Human factors in computing systems*, New York, NY, USA, 2009, pp. 1589-1598.

[5]   Buckley J., O'Brien M. P., and Power N., "Empirically Refining a Model of Programmers' Information-Seeking Behavior During Software Maintenance," in *Romero, P., Good, J., Acosta Chaparro E. and Bryant S. (Eds). Proceedings of the 18th Workshop of the Psychology of Programming Interest Group*, 2006, pp. 168-182.

[6]   Case D. O., *Looking for Information: A Survey of Research on Information Seeking, Needs, and Behavior.* Burlington: Elsevier, 2006.

[7]   Chatterjee S., Juvekar S., and Sen K., "Sniff: A Search Engine for Java Using Free-Form Queries," in *Proceedings of the 12th International Conference on Fundamental Approaches to Software Engineering*, Berlin/Heidelberg, 2009, pp. 385-400.

[8]   Chen W., Li J., Ma J., Conradi R., Ji J., and Liu C., "An Empirical Study on Software Development with Open Source Components in the Chinese Software Industry," *Software Process: Improvement and Practice,* vol. 13, p. 12, 2008.

[9]   Choo C. W., Detlor B., and Turnbull D., *Web Work: Information Seeking and Knowledge Work on the World Wide Web*. Amsterdam, The Netherlands: Kluwer Academic Publishers, 2000.

[10]   Cottrell R., Walker R. J., and Denzinger J., "Jigsaw: A Tool for the Small-Scale Reuse of Source Code," in *Companion of the 30th international conference on Software engineering*, New York, NY, USA, 2008, pp. 933-934.

[11]   Coverity, Coverity Scan Open Source Report, 2009, http://www.coverity.com/scan/ [December 2009].

[12]   Dagenais B. and Ossher H., "Automatically Locating Framework Extension Examples," New York, NY, USA, 2008, pp. 203-213.

[13]   Dix A., Finlay J., Abowd G. D., and Beale R., *Human-Computer Interaction. Second Edition.* Upper Saddle River, NJ, USA: Prentice Hall, 1998.

[14]   Durao F. A., Vanderlei T. A., Almeida E. S., and de L. Meira S. R., "Applying a Semantic Layer in a Source Code Search Tool," in *Proceedings of the 2008 ACM symposium on Applied computing*, New York, NY, USA, 2008, pp. 1151-1157.

[15]   Ellis D. and Haugan M., "Modelling the Information Seeking Patterns of Engineers and Research Scientists in an Industrial Environment," *Journal of Documentation*, vol. 53, pp. 384-403, 1997.

[16]   Gallardo-Valencia R. E. and Sim S. E., "Internet-Scale Code Search," in *Proceedings of the 2009 ICSE Workshop on Search-Driven Development-Users, Infrastructure, Tools and Evaluation*, Washington, DC, USA, 2009, pp. 49-52.

[17]   Garcia V., Lucredio D., Durao F., Santos E., Almeida E., Fortes R., and Meira S., "From Specification to Experimentation: A Software Component Search Engine Architecture," *Lecture notes in computer science*, vol. 4063, pp. 82-97, 2006.

[18]   Gartner, Gartner Highlights Key Predictions for It Organisations and Users in 2008 and Beyond, 2008, http://www.gartner.com/it/page.jsp?id=593207 [December 2009].

[19]   Goldman M. and Miller R. C., "Codetrail: Connecting Source Code and Web Resources," *Journal of Visual Languages & Computing. Special Issue on Best Papers from VL/HCC 2008,* vol. 20, pp. 223-235, 2009.

[20]   Hassan A. E., "Mining Software Repositories to Assist Developers and Support Managers," in *Proceedings of the 22nd IEEE International Conference on Software Maintenance*, Los Alamitos,CA,USA, 2006, pp. 339-342.

[21]   Hoffmann R., Fogarty J., and Weld D. S., "Assieme: Finding and Leveraging Implicit References in a Web Search Interface for Programmers," in *Proceedings of the 20th annual ACM symposium on User interface software and technology*, New York, NY, USA, 2007.

[22]   Holmes R. and Walker R. J., "Supporting the Investigation and Planning of Pragmatic Reuse Tasks," in *Proceedings of the 29th International Conference on Software Engineering*, Washington, DC, USA, 2007, pp. 447-457.

[23]   Holmes R., Walker R. J., and Murphy G. C., "Approximate Structural Context Matching: An Approach to Recommend Relevant Examples," *IEEE Transactions on Software Engineering*, vol. 32, pp. 952-970, 2006.

[24]   Hughes H., "Responses and Influences: A Model of Online Information Use for Learning," *Information Research*, vol. 12, paper 279, 2006 http://informationr.net/ir/12-1/paper279.html [November 2009].

[25] Hughes H., Bruce C., and Edwards S., "Fostering a Reflective Approach to Online Information Use for Learning," in *Proceedings of the 4th International Lifelong Learning Conference. Lifelong Learning: Partners, Pathways, and Pedagogies*, Rockhampton, Australia, 2006, pp. 143-150.

[26] Hummel O. and Atkinson C., "Extreme Harvesting: Test Driven Discovery and Reuse of Software Components," in *Proceedings of the 2004 IEEE International Conference on Information Reuse and Integration*, 2004, pp. 66-72.

[27] Hummel O. and Atkinson C., "Using the Web as a Reuse Repository," *Lecture notes in computer science*, vol. 4039, pp. 298-311, 2006.

[28] Hummel O., Janjic W., and Atkinson C., "Code Conjurer: Pulling Reusable Software out of Thin Air," *IEEE Software*, vol. 25, pp. 45-52, 2008.

[29] Inoue K., Yokomori R., Yamamoto T., Matsushita M., and Kusumoto S., "Ranking Significance of Software Components Based on Use Relations," *IEEE Transactions on Software Engineering*, vol. 31, pp. 213-225, 2005.

[30] International Organization for Standarization ISO, *Iso/Iec Standard 9126: Software Engineering - Product Quality, Part 1*, 2001.

[31] Ko A. J., DeLine R., and Venolia G., "Information Needs in Collocated Software Development Teams," in *Proceedings of the 29th international conference on Software Engineering*, Washington, DC, USA, 2007, pp. 344-353.

[32] Krueger C. W., "Software Reuse," *ACM Computing Surveys*, vol. 24, pp. 131-183, 1992.

[33] Kuhlthau C. C., "Inside the Search Process: Information Seeking from the User's Perspective," *Journal of the American Society for Information Science*, vol. 42, pp. 361-371, 1991.

[34] Lavoie B. and Nielsen H. F., Web Characterization Terminology and Definitions Sheet. W3c Working Draft, World Wide Web Consortium (W3c), 1999, http://www.w3.org/1999/05/WCA-terms/ [November 2009].

[35] Lazzarini Lemos O. A., Bajracharya S., Ossher J., Masiero P. C., and Lopes C., "Applying Test-Driven Code Search to the Reuse of Auxiliary Functionality," in *Proceedings of the 2009 ACM symposium on Applied Computing*, New York, NY, USA, 2009, pp. 476-482.

[36] Linstead E., Bajracharya S., Ngo T., Rigor P., Lopes C., and Baldi P., "Sourcerer: Mining and Searching Internet-Scale Software Repositories," *Data Mining and Knowledge Discovery*, vol. 18, pp. 300-336, 2009.

[37] Madanmohan T. R. and De' R., "Open Source Reuse in Commercial Firms," *IEEE Software*, vol. 21, pp. 62-69, 2004.

[38] Mandelin D., Xu L., Bodik R., and Kimelman D., "Jungloid Mining: Helping to Navigate the Api Jungle," *ACM SIGPLAN Notices*, vol. 40, pp. 48-61, 2005.

[39]   Marchionini G., *Information Seeking in Electronic Environments*. New York, NY, USA: Cambridge University Press, 1997.

[40]   Marchionini G., "Exploratory Search: From Finding to Understanding," *Communications of ACM*, vol. 49, pp. 41-46, 2006.

[41]   McCarey F., Cinneide M. O., and Kushmerick N., "Knowledge Reuse for Software Reuse," *Web Intelligence Agent Systems*, vol. 6, pp. 59-81, 2008.

[42]   O'Brien M. P. and Buckley J., "Modelling the Information-Seeking Behaviour of Programmers - an Empirical Approach," in *Proceedings of the 13th International Workshop on Program Comprehension (IWPC'05)*, Los Alamitos, CA, USA, 2005, pp. 125-134.

[43]   Pearsall J. and Trumble B., The Oxford English Reference Dictionary, Second ed. Oxford, England: Oxford University Press, 1996.

[44]   Pirolli P. and Card S., "Information Foraging in Information Access Environments," in *Proceedings of the SIGCHI conference on Human factors in computing systems*, New York, NY, USA, 1995, pp. 51-58.

[45]   Poshyvanyk D., Marcus A., and Dong Y., "Jiriss - an Eclipse Plug-in for Source Code Exploration," in *Proceedings of the 14th IEEE International Conference on Program Comprehension*, Los Alamitos, CA, USA, 2006, pp. 252-255.

[46]   Reiss S. P., "Semantics-Based Code Search," in *Proceedings of the 2009 IEEE 31st International Conference on Software Engineering*, Washington, DC, USA, 2009, pp. 243-253.

[47]   Sahavechaphan N. and Claypool K., "Xsnippet: Mining for Sample Code," *ACM SIGPLAN Notices*, vol. 41, pp. 413-430, 2006.

[48]   Seacord R. C., Hissam S. A., and Wallnau K. C., "Agora: A Search Engine for Software Components," *IEEE Internet Computing*, vol. 2, pp. 62-70, 1998.

[49]   Sharif K. Y. and Buckley J., "Observing Open Source Programmers' Information Seeking," in *Proceedings of the 20th Workshop of the Psychology of Programming Interest Group*, 2008, pp. 7-16.

[50]   Sim S. E., Clarke C. L. A., and Holt R. C., "Archetypal Source Code Searches: A Survey of Software Developers and Maintainers," in *Proceedings of the 6th International Workshop on Program Comprehension*, Washington, DC, USA, 1998, pp. 180-187.

[51]   Sim S. E., Umarji M., Ratanotayanon S., and Lopes C. V., "How Well Do Internet Code Search Engines Support Open Source Reuse Strategies?," *ACM Transactions on Software Engineering and Methodologies*, 2009. *In submission*.

[52]   Sindhgatta R., "Using an Information Retrieval System to Retrieve Source Code Samples," in *Proceedings of the 28th international conference on Software engineering*, New York, NY, USA, 2006, pp. 905-908.

[53]   Solomon M. R., *Consumer Behavior. Buying, Having, and Being.*, Eighth ed. New Jersey: Pearson, 2009.

[54]   Storey M. A., "Theories, Methods and Tools in Program Comprehension: Past, Present and Future," in *Proceedings of the 13th International Workshop on Program Comprehension*, Los Alamitos, CA, USA, 2005, pp. 181-191.

[55]   Stylos J. and Myers B. A., "Mica: A Web-Search Tool for Finding Api Components and Examples," in *Proceedings of the Visual Languages and Human-Centric Computing*, Washington, DC, USA, 2006, pp. 195-202.

[56]   Sutcliffe A. and Ennis M., "Towards a Cognitive Theory of Information Retrieval," *Interacting with Computers*, vol. 10, pp. 321-351, 1998.

[57]   Taylor R. S., "Question-Negotiation and Information Seeking in Libraries," *College & Research Libraries*, vol. 29, pp. 178-194, 1968.

[58]   Thummalapenta S. and Xie T., "Parseweb: A Programmer Assistant for Reusing Open Source Code on the Web," in *Proceedings of 22nd IEEE/ACM international conference on Automated software engineering*, New York, NY, USA, 2007, pp. 204-213.

[59]   Umarji M., Sim S. E., and Lopes C., "Archetypal Internet-Scale Source Code Searching," in *Ifip International Federation for Information Processing, Volume 275: Open Source Development, Communities and Quality*, B. Russo, E. Damiani, S. Hissam, B. Lundell, and G. Succi, Eds. Boston: Springer, 2008, pp. 257-263.

[60]   van der Berg K., "Finding Open Options. An Open Source Software Evaluation Model with a Case Study on Course Management Systems," Master Degree Thesis, Tilburg University, 2005.

[61]   van Vliet H., *Software Engineering: Principles and Practice. Third Edition*. Chichester, UK: Wiley, 2008.

[62]   Vanderlei T. A., Durao F. A., Martins A. C., Garcia V. C., Almeida E. S., and de L. Meira S. R., "A Cooperative Classification Mechanism for Search and Retrieval Software Components," in *Proceedings of the 2007 ACM Symposium on Applied Computing*, New York, NY, USA, 2007, pp. 866-871.

[63]   Wilson T. D., "Information Behaviour: An Interdisciplinary Perspective," *Information Processing & Management*, vol. 33, pp. 551-572, 1997.

[64]   Wilson T. D., "Models in Information Behaviour Research," *Journal of Documentation*, vol. 55, pp. 249-270, 1999.

[65]   Xie T. and Pei J., "Mapo: Mining Api Usages from Open Source Repositories," in *Proceedings of the 2006 International Workshop on Mining Software Repositories*, New York, NY, USA, 2006, pp. 54-57.

[66]   Ye Y. and Fischer G., "Supporting Reuse by Delivering Task-Relevant and Personalized Information," in *Proceedings of the 24th International Conference on Software Engineering*, New York, NY, USA, 2002, pp. 513-523.

[67]   Ye Y., Yamamoto Y., Nakakoji K., Nishinaka Y., and Asada M., "Searching the Library and Asking the Peers: Learning to Use Java Apis on Demand," in *Proceedings of the 5th International Symposium on Principles and Practice of Programming in Java*, New York, NY, USA, 2007, pp. 41-50.

[68]   Zhang J., *Visualization for Information Retrieval : The Information Retrieval Series*. Berlin, Germany: Springer, 2008.